GOD'S GRACE APART FROM LAW

D1475003

MICK MOONEY

God's Grace Apart From Law

A conversational journey through the first three chapters of Paul's letter to the Romans

Mick Mooney

Other Books By Mick Mooney

Non-Fiction

Look! The Finished Work Of Jesus

Paraphrase

The Gospel Cannot Be Chained

Comic Book

Searching For Grace: Joining The Church

LĬGHTVIEW MEDIA

Dedicated to all who believe in the incomparable
power of God's grace

Table Of Contents

INTRODUCTION

Paul's letter to the Roman Church is, in a nutshell, a testimony of God's grace: the Gospel of God. It brings into focus not only the correct way to understand the New Covenant reality of grace, but also, perhaps more significantly, the correct way to understand the Old Covenant of law. The importance of this clarification cannot be understated. In fact, it was the dominant theme Paul continued to clarify to the church throughout his entire known ministry. To Paul, the Christian life was lived through the profound reality of grace.

The New Covenant is the awakening of God's divine way of the Spirit, established at its appointed time through the finished work of his Son.[1] Paul was convinced of this new era of grace, and, in a way that perhaps only Paul could do, he explained how all things found their reality in grace and how all things are achieved through the power

---

[1] He has made us competent as ministers of a new covenant—not of the letter but of the Spirit; for the letter kills, but the Spirit gives life. **2 Corinthians 3:6**

of grace. Grace was not merely a nice word to Paul; *it was the very nature of God*. It was to Paul, and remains true for every generation, the all-encompassing power of the Almighty.

Some, in Paul's day, thought 'grace' was a word thrown around in Christian circles to excuse someone's failings; Paul understood it as the very essence of the empowered Christian life. The message he shared, when we search for its foundations in Scripture, is evident. However, in Paul's day it was, and still is to this day, a revolutionary message that many in the church simply could not bring themselves to accept. They preferred to dismiss Paul and his understanding of the gospel as one not worthy to be listened to. That is a sad situation indeed as God called Paul specifically so the church could and would embrace the message he shared. While it was Jesus' unique ministry to *establish* the reality of grace for all of us, it was Paul's unique ministry to *explain* the reality of grace in words we, as the church, could grasp.[2]

In fact, at least once after his resurrection, Jesus needed to speak directly to one of his early disciples to clarify that, indeed, it was God himself who had appointed Paul as his 'chosen instrument' to bring the reality of the gospel message to the world.[3] The Apostle Paul, as the unique instrument chosen by God, was given the revelation of God's good news directly into his spirit. Paul himself testifies about this reality in his letter to the Galatians:

---

[2] Although I am less than the least of all God's people, this grace was given me: to preach to the Gentiles the unsearchable riches of Christ, and to make plain to everyone the administration of this mystery, which for ages past was kept hidden in God, who created all things. **Ephesians 3:8-9**

[3] But the Lord said to Ananias, "Go! This man is my chosen instrument to proclaim my name to the Gentiles and their kings and to the people of Israel." **Acts 9:15**

4

I want you to know, brothers, that the gospel I preached is not something that man made up. I did not receive it from any man, nor was I taught it; rather, I received it by revelation from Jesus Christ. ***Galatians 1:11-12***

If Paul received this message of good news that he so passionately preached directly from Jesus then it's certainly a good idea to take hold of the gospel that Paul preached and embrace it, love it, and live in it. This is, in fact, the very reason Paul was given such an amazing revelation of the gospel in the first place; it was for the benefit of the body of Christ.[4] In fact, even the Apostle Peter, who walked with Jesus for three years and was closer to Jesus in his earthly ministry than anyone else, encouraged the church to listen to Paul's message.

Bear in mind that our Lord's patience means salvation, just as our dear brother Paul also wrote you with the wisdom that God gave him. He writes the same way in all his letters, speaking in them of these matters. His letters contain some things that are hard to understand, which ignorant and unstable people distort, as they do the other Scriptures, to their own destruction. ***2 Peter 3:15-16***

The reason Paul preached the gospel so passionately was so Christ's body, his church, would discover their promised rest in it.

---

[4] Now I rejoice in what was suffered for you, and I fill up in my flesh what is still lacking in regard to Christ's afflictions, for the sake of his body, which is the church. I have become its servant by the commission God gave me to present to you the word of God in its fullness— the mystery that has been kept hidden for ages and generations, but is now disclosed to the saints. **Colossians 1:24-26**

According to Paul's own testimony towards the end of the book of Acts, it was his divine mandate to preach this wonderful good news:

However, I consider my life worth nothing to me, if only I may finish the race and complete the task the Lord Jesus has given me—the task of testifying to the gospel of God's grace. Acts 20:24

Everything Paul did was, in one way or another, connected to this one goal: to testify to the gospel of God's grace. We see Paul doing this in all his letters; however, nowhere does he lay out the nuts and bolts of the gospel of God's grace as systematically as he does in his letter to the Romans. Why did Paul do such a thing? Was it to prove to the world that he was a wise and learned scholar? I doubt anyone would conclude that. In fact, I don't think anyone would judge Paul's motives as self-gratifying. On the contrary, for it seems evident that Paul wouldn't have found any personal satisfaction in being known for his academic credentials. His boast was not in what he knew; but rather, in the profound reality that he was known and loved by God.[5] It was this reality that consumed his attention; he found his peace in the grace of our great God. Paul didn't seek to identify himself as a theologian; rather, he identified himself as a child of God radically set free 'in Christ'.

Paul doesn't give us the impression through his life and letters to the early church that he was interested in the theories of God. To Paul the gospel wasn't a theory. He lived his life out of a revelation

---

[5] I have been crucified with Christ and I no longer live, but Christ lives in me. The life I live in the body, I live by faith in the Son of God, who loved me and gave himself for me. **Galatians 2:20**

of Christ. He lived with a foundational belief that the good news of God's grace was a profound and living reality in his life; a reality so glorious that it made everything else pale by comparison.[6] He didn't get caught up in side issues. He fought passionately to keep the focus of our faith upon the glorious reality of Jesus and the new creation life that was given through his death and resurrection.

He lived to proclaim the greatness of Christ and the power of his perfect, finished work on the cross. He lived to keep the church focused on Jesus and he knew the only way that would function was when the church was firmly grounded in the good news of God's grace. This is the same task we endeavour to do today; to keep our hearts focused on Jesus and our spirits founded in his grace. We too can live with the understanding that God's grace is not a theory or a doctrine; *it's a profound and glorious reality*. It's good to know that our lives are not based on lifeless theological words. They're based on the living Christ, on his person, and on his reality.

Paul exemplified how receiving the understanding of God's way of the Spirit and being able to express it to others has no correlation with one's intellectual capacity to express theological concepts with large and complicated religious words. Other preachers of Paul's day purposely slandered him because he refused to speak in academic terminology. Paul didn't find this an insult but rather he was pleased that his message could be presented to all people regardless of their education. Like Paul, we can also be encouraged that we don't

---

[6] But whatever was to my profit I now consider loss for the sake of Christ. What is more, I consider everything a loss compared to the surpassing greatness of knowing Christ Jesus my Lord, for whose sake I have lost all things. I consider them rubbish, that I may gain Christ and be found in him, not having a righteousness of my own that comes from the law, but that which is through faith in Christ—the righteousness that comes from God and is by faith. **Philippians 3:7-9**

need to get caught up in using big theological words and quoting other academic works. Through the help of the Spirit Paul managed to share the most profound revelation in all of eternity in a way that his listeners, from the farmers to the ruling class, could understand.

Now this is our boast: Our conscience testifies that we have conducted ourselves in the world, and especially in our relations with you, in the holiness and sincerity that are from God. We have done so not according to worldly wisdom but according to God's grace. For we do not write you anything you cannot read or understand.
2 Corinthians 1:12-13

Unfortunately when a Christian tries to fit Paul's letters into the theology of a mixed covenant of law and grace, it not only becomes difficult to understand Paul's letters but it actually becomes impossible. Paul often described how other preachers of his day were determined to make Christians submit also to the Jewish law. These preachers taught the importance of specific Old Covenant laws as a continual requirement for Christian living in order to receive God's covenant blessings. Although Paul makes reference to this group in many of his letters, he addresses them the most pointedly in his letter to the Galatians. He directly challenged their false gospel. According to the gospel of God's grace that Jesus gave Paul to preach, a Christian is not under the law nor is God blessing or cursing a Christian depending upon their obedience to a written code.

These other preachers, alternatively, were preaching a contradictory message. They were actually trying to convince the church it was through following certain Old Covenant laws that they would be blessed and considered obedient in God's eyes. It is important to point out that these preachers were not simply Jewish teachers who had rejected Jesus and were trying to discredit Christianity or seeking to convert believers to Judaism; on the contrary, they were very much a part of the body of Christ, or at the very least, presented themselves publicly as active Christian teachers; however, they had a determined zeal to keep some of the laws found in the Old Covenant as part of the New Covenant.

They preached about Jesus, the cross, and the resurrection; however, when it came to the important foundation of the gospel being grace alone apart from the law, rather than preaching the truth of the New Covenant, of grace apart from law, they went their own way and preached their own distorted message of a mixed covenant. Because of this they ended up actually preaching a different gospel than God ever intended to be preached. This resulted in the churches in Galatia and elsewhere believing in a different Jesus. No longer was Jesus thought of as the One who offered them rest in his presence; but rather, now Jesus was thought of as even stricter than Moses, watching and waiting for obedience to Old Covenant laws as his motivation to give his blessings. No longer was Jesus someone they connected directly with through the Spirit; instead, they started believing in a Jesus who expected them to submit to mediators, these mixed covenant preachers, who enforced an unquestionable 'spiritual authority' over the church.

For if someone comes to you and preaches a Jesus other than the Jesus we preached, or if you receive a different spirit from the Spirit you received, or a different gospel from the one you accepted, you put up with it easily enough. **2 *Corinthians 11:4***

Paul went to extreme measures to highlight just how significant and devastating this false teaching was, going so far as to say that it was actually disabling the grace empowered life within them.

It is for freedom that Christ has set us free. Stand firm, then, and do not let yourselves be burdened again by a yoke of slavery. Mark my words! I, Paul, tell you that if you let yourselves be circumcised, Christ will be of no value to you at all. Again I declare to every man who lets himself be circumcised that he is obligated to obey the whole law. You who are trying to be justified by the law have been alienated from Christ; you have fallen away from grace. ***Galatians 5:1-4***

Although Paul specifically mentions circumcision in his example, the same can be said for any Old Covenant law that a Christian tries to religiously follow today. The bottom line is if you want to follow one of them then you must be prepared to follow all of them. Of course this is impossible; however, that is the point. We should not be religiously holding onto the observance of any Old Covenant laws nor should we submit ourselves to those determined to yoke us to them.

What we need to remember is that we, in Christ, are new creations who live out of the very DNA of love. We live not by legalistic rules but by a Spirit radically alive within us.[7] This means

---

[7] Because those who are led by the Spirit of God are sons of God. For you did not receive a spirit that makes you a slave again to fear, but you received the Spirit of sonship. And by him we cry, *"Abba,* Father." **Romans 8:14-15**

that anything that is of love we will naturally desire to walk in. We don't kill because we love. We don't steal because we love. It is love and not laws that motivates our actions as New Covenant believers. This love can be trusted for it is founded in the Spirit of the divine God living in us. There is a difference, however, between actions of love and obligations of law. When we fail to understand the difference we live our lives in guilt instead of in our true inheritance of grace. God doesn't desire for you to live a mixed life of guilt and grace. He desires you to be truly free, alive, and active in his grace alone.[8]

When a Christian sits under a mixed covenant teaching for long enough and, as Paul says, *"puts up with it easily enough,"* they can, like the churches in Galatia, truly start living in confusion and never grasp the reality of their God given right to find their rest in his grace. Instead they find themselves on a religious performance tread mill and end up spending their time striving to receive from God based by what they do instead of freely receiving everything from him based on his love.[9] The foundational truth of the New Covenant is one of grace.

We don't receive good things from God based on our works; rather, we receive everything based on the perfect work of Jesus, the creator of the universe, the King of kings and the Lord of Lords. He is the one who created all things and through whom all things are held together – and he is graceful. The eternal purpose of everything in the

---

[8] It is for freedom that Christ has set us free. Stand firm, then, and do not let yourselves be burdened again by a yoke of slavery. **Galatians 5:1**

[9] You foolish Galatians! Who has bewitched you? Before your very eyes Jesus Christ was clearly portrayed as crucified. I would like to learn just one thing from you: Did you receive the Spirit by observing the law, or by believing what you heard? Are you so foolish? After beginning with the Spirit, are you now trying to attain your goal by human effort? Have you suffered so much for nothing—if it really was for nothing? **Galatians 3:1-4**

heart of God is found and finished in the life of Jesus, the sacrifice he made on the cross, and the result of the new life that comes out of that sacrifice. This is our reality. This is the gospel. This is the good news that could only ever be given through a pure act of God's grace for how could man ever earn such a blessing? It is for this reason that we don't try to *earn* such a wonderful reality; rather, we rejoice in the *gift* of this precious good news. It is our inheritance in Christ: the good news of God's grace.

Paul's letter helped the early church then, and it continues to help the church today, to understand how God's grace is more than enough to bring about God's righteousness, obedience, and the Christ empowered life to every believer. Paul's intention in writing this letter was to encourage the church in this wonderful reality of grace.

I

PAUL'S HEART AND MOTIVES

As Paul makes clear in his opening greetings, his letter was written to the church in Rome. Unlike Paul's letters to the other churches, this church was not personally founded by him. However, it was most likely founded by someone he personally knew and trusted. Although Paul had never visited the church in Rome, he did have some pre-existing friendships with several members which were evident from his personal greetings at the end of his letter. He was most likely asked by some of these friends to write to the church in Rome to clarify the profound reality of both God's grace as well as the true reality of the Law of Moses and its true purpose within the eternal plan of God. We could confidently say that the overarching purpose of Paul's letter was to help the church in Rome understand the relationship between law and grace.

Throughout his letter Paul presented the gospel of God's grace, keeping a focus on the finished work of Jesus, and also addressed some misunderstandings that many in the church had regarding the interpretation and purpose of the law. He wrote to encourage the church and ultimately to help them understand the foundational truth that had been given to them through the gospel. The foundation is that there is not only forgiveness of sins by the grace of God but the gift of all things godly are given by grace: including righteousness, obedience, a fruitful life, good works, freedom from sin, love, holiness, and anything else that comes from the heart of God. All things in Christ are assured to the believer because they are a *gift* that comes through the grace of God. Indeed, according to Paul's revelation, all roads lead to grace.

Righteousness is a major theme Paul addresses in his letter and he does this knowing that many sincere, well-meaning members of the church had a wrong understanding on what righteousness was and how a believer is considered righteous in God's eyes. To many in the church, it seemed only natural to assume that the way a Christian could live out a good and God pleasing life was to read and obey the law that God had given the Israelites in the Old Covenant. After all the God of the New Covenant was also the God of the Old Covenant and everyone knew that God did not change. Paul agreed that God did not suddenly change but he didn't see a God of law who carried over into the new idea of grace. He saw a God who had always been about grace now fully revealing the mystery of his true nature within the New Covenant. He understood what was concealed in the Old Testament was now being powerfully revealed in the New.[10] His goal was to help his readers understand they could view God and his righteousness looking through the enlightened reality of the New Covenant instead of straining to see through the dim shadow of the Old Covenant.

Paul makes the bold assumption that it was only now through the life, death, and resurrection of Jesus that God's reality of righteousness is revealed to all mankind. It had always been attested to in the Old Testament and it had indeed been promised but it was only through Jesus that it was fully revealed and brought to light. It was a beautiful reality that nobody was able to fully see or fully grasp in the Old Testament but it had, nonetheless, always been there. Paul also testifies to this in the climax of his introduction in this letter:

For in the gospel a righteousness from God is revealed, a righteousness that is by faith from first to last, just as it is written: "The righteous will live by faith." **Romans 1:17**

Paul was helping the church to understand a profound reality and the blessedness given to all who are in Christ. We are now living in a New Covenant in which we receive God's righteousness as a gift of his grace and not as a payment for obeying a written code of rules. This was a very difficult aspect of God's divine truth for many of the members of the church to grasp, especially those who had a Jewish heritage because it was a massive paradigm shift in how to interpret what God had been doing throughout the Old Testament. It was also

---

[10] We are not like Moses, who would put a veil over his face to keep the Israelites from gazing at it while the radiance was fading away. But their minds were made dull, for to this day the same veil remains when the old covenant is read. It has not been removed, because only in Christ is it taken away. **2 Corinthians 3:13-14**

difficult for the Gentiles in the church who had a religious bent to their personality, who liked the idea of the Jewish God of law, and also wanted to embrace this history as their own.

Paul, of course, was not against the Jews. He himself had a Jewish heritage. What he wanted to do was help his fellow brothers who shared the same heritage as he did to step fully into the New Covenant and embrace the reality of Christ even though it required letting go of their false understanding of the law. That false belief taught that the law was a useful and effective tool for teaching Christians to live a righteous life; however, as Paul clarifies throughout many of his letters, nothing could be further from the gospel truth![11] It is the revelation of grace that empowers a believer to live a righteous life; in contrast, the law will only create condemnation and a feeling of unworthiness that pushes a believer into sin. Paul said it was grace and not law that would liberate us into an obedient and righteous life.

For sin shall not be your master, because you are not under law, but under grace. **Romans 6:14**

We should also take note as we begin this journey to recognise that the Roman church was not going the wrong way in their faith. They were actually commended as being a church community full of faith. Their challenge, however, was that they had not yet grasped in their minds the fullness of their New Covenant inheritance. Paul was ultimately trying to help them understand in their minds the reality of God's grace apart from law in order that their spirits could

---

[11] Before this faith came, we were held prisoners by the law, locked up until faith should be revealed. So the law was put in charge to lead us to Christ that we might be justified by faith. Now that faith has come, we are no longer under the supervision of the law. **Galatians 3:23-25**

fully rest in it. I believe that the almighty power of God's grace apart from man's willpower and determination is something that every Christian inherently understands in their new creation spirit. However, when we cannot reconcile this with the religious assumption that we are also required to live up to the written code of God's righteous ideal, it weakens our own foundations in our faith because we mix our own failed works into the reality of Christ's finished work done on our behalf. The divine foundation in Christ is one of pure grace. It's a radical thought; however, it is completely heavenly in truth.

Paul's task through writing this letter was to explain, in a way that the church could grasp, how that God in fact never defined righteousness as something that could be obtained by following a written code of rules and regulations. God wasn't suddenly and drastically changing his mind on the whole topic of righteousness; rather, Paul made the claim that it was, in fact, Israel who had misunderstood God's reason for giving them the law in the first place. They failed to recognise *God's true intention* for the law resulting in them setting up *their own purpose* for the law and their own definition of righteousness; one that comes through obeying a written code even though this was never God's intention. As Paul testifies:

Brothers, my heart's desire and prayer to God for the Israelites is that they may be saved. For I can testify about them that they are zealous for God, but their zeal is not based on knowledge. Since they did not know the righteousness that comes from God and sought to establish their own, they did not submit to God's righteousness. Christ is the end of the law so that there may be righteousness for everyone who believes. **Romans 10:1-4**

The truth that Paul revealed to the church was that God never intended the law to be a written code that man could follow to obtain a standing of righteousness in God's eyes; but rather, that the law was given to lead people to the one and only person who could impart righteousness to them as a pure act of grace on his part; the man Jesus Christ!

What, then, was the purpose of the law? It was added because of transgressions until the Seed to whom the promise referred had come. **Galatians 3:19**

So the law was put in charge to lead us to Christ that we might be justified by faith. Now that faith has come, we are no longer under the supervision of the law. **Galatians 3:24-25**

Misunderstanding God's true intentions for the law leads a Christian to take upon themselves the religious yoke of a work's based righteousness. This often results in the compulsion to defend the Old Covenant law as a continual obligation for Christian living. This doesn't come out of an impure motive but rather a misplaced mindset. When Christians do not understand in their minds that they are not obligated to the law, they are hindered from fully embracing their divine union with the grace of God. This false understanding of the law's purpose in their life causes a conflict within them and hinders them from fully embracing the full freedom and blessedness of being a new creation in Christ.

Paul was a spiritual man. He wanted the church to live by the spirit and not by their rational minds but he also understood the stronghold that was in their minds. It was this stronghold Paul endeavoured to free the church in Rome from.[12] This was Paul's heart for the church in Rome and, ultimately, it is God's heart for the church collectively in Christ. God's desire is that we too would be willing to renew our minds so that we can truly live in the good news of God's grace apart from law. Paul goes through this letter explaining, somewhat systematically, the history of God's walk with people, both Israel and Gentiles, in order to outline God's divine and eternal reality.

Paul's desire was to show the fullness and this reality to his brothers and sisters in Rome and reveal the true purpose of the law: that it was, in fact, never given as a means of righteousness. Although to the religious mind it seems right to cling to the law, Paul was pointing out that it is a misplaced belief to have and it will only cause us to neglect the true power unto righteousness. It is a *gift* of God's grace.[13] He showed through his letter to the Romans that we all need to let go of the religious mindset that exalts the law and in its place embrace the mind of Christ that exalts the working of God's grace in us.

Everyone who has been made new in Christ has been given the mind of Christ and Christ's mind is a mind that is full of the reality

---

[12] Do not conform to the pattern of this world, but be transformed by the renewing of your mind. Then you will be able to test and approve what God's will is—his good, pleasing and perfect will. **Romans 12:2**

[13] For if, by the trespass of the one man, death reigned through that one man, how much more will those who receive God's abundant provision of grace and of the gift of righteousness reign in life through the one man, Jesus Christ. **Romans 5:17**

of the grace of God. Jesus came full of grace and truth. His mind is full of grace and truth and that is the mind we have inherited through him. Let us embrace the mind of Christ and the fullness of his grace as we take this journey through the letter to the Romans.

"For who has known the mind of the Lord that he may instruct him?" But we have the mind of Christ. **1 Corinthians 2:16**

II

What Is The Gospel?

Paul, a servant of Christ Jesus, called to be an apostle and set apart for the gospel of God. **Romans 1:1**

Paul starts his letter by explaining his commission from God that he was called and set apart to preach the gospel of God. Before we go any further on our journey it's worth asking the question; *what is the gospel of God?*

In the Scriptures we read the gospel mentioned by Jesus, Paul, Peter, John, and the other authors with many different titles attached to its ending. It's called the gospel of peace, the gospel of salvation, the gospel of the kingdom, the eternal gospel, the gospel of God, and the gospel of God's Son. Does this mean that these are all different gospels? Are there many gospels? Well, not according to the Apostle Paul. He assures us in his letter to the Galatians that there is in fact only one gospel:

I am astonished that you are so quickly deserting the one who called you by the grace of Christ and are turning to a different gospel — which is really no gospel at all. **Galatians 1:6-7**

Although it is possible for many false gospels to be preached, there is only one true gospel. With this in mind, we can read once again Paul's declaration to the Ephesian elders recorded at the end of the book of Acts to understand the very essence of the gospel which is that the one, all-encompassing characteristic of the gospel is God's grace:

However, I consider my life worth nothing to me, if only I may finish the race and complete the task the Lord Jesus has given me—the task of testifying to the gospel of God's grace. **Acts 20:24**

Paul's divine commission was to be set apart in order to preach and testify about the gospel of God's grace. That is the gospel – the only gospel. When we, as Christians, think that Jesus' *'gospel of the kingdom'* was somehow different to Paul's *'gospel of God's grace'* we end up not only confusing ourselves but also our listeners. The truth is that God's kingdom is God's grace. God's entire kingdom is founded upon his grace. God sits on a throne of grace.[14] The Holy Spirit is the Spirit of grace. Jesus came full of grace!

Jesus entered into a religious world that threw the term *'kingdom'* around all the time as a way of judging the world and coercing others to get involved with their religious programs. Jesus

---

[14] Let us then approach the throne of grace with confidence, so that we may receive mercy and find grace to help us in our time of need. **Hebrews 4:16**

took that same term and presented the *'kingdom'* not as a physical place on earth but rather as it truly is; an internal reality.[15]

The revelation of the kingdom is not about man's morals but about God's grace. For out of his grace all good and moral things can come to pass. The message of the kingdom *is* the message that God is the God of all grace. That is the message Jesus preached and through Jesus this grace reality is freely available for all who believe. God's kingdom is not something external *that we* need to work towards establishing for him; however, it is something internal *that he* has already established in us.

Grace is the very nature of God. It is God's nature that had always been misunderstood and rejected by mankind but now is revealed and finally embraced through the life of Christ. It is only through seeing the fullness of what Jesus did on our behalf and understanding that this was actually God that we can embrace the reality of God himself. The truth of God is that grace is his nature. God's Spirit is a Spirit of grace. Grace is the very power that God has placed into every believer to empower them in life. We now have grace which is the empowering nature of God living in us.

Jesus revealed the gospel of God's grace through his life, his teaching, and ultimately his sacrifice upon the cross. It was Paul's task then to reveal that same gospel in words that we, the church, could grasp and understand. Jesus lived in the reality of God's grace giving

---

[15] Then Jesus asked, "What is the kingdom of God like? What shall I compare it to? It is like a mustard seed, which a man took and planted in his garden. It grew and became a tree, and the birds of the air perched in its branches." **Luke 13:18-19**

Once, having been asked by the Pharisees when the kingdom of God would come, Jesus replied, "The kingdom of God does not come with your careful observation, nor will people say, 'Here it is,' or 'There it is,' because the kingdom of God is within you." **Luke 17:20-21**

us the example of what a person's life looks like that knows without a doubt that they are loved by their heavenly Father, that they are one with him, and that he is pleased with them.

Jesus ultimately went on to establish the opportunity for all of us to also live in this glorious reality through his sacrifice and resurrection. After the resurrection Jesus set Paul apart, a man who could have only become an apostle by grace, to make clear to the church this incredible good news. Paul also testifies to this in his final remarks to the church in Rome:

Now to him who is able to establish you by my gospel and the proclamation of Jesus Christ, according to the revelation of the mystery hidden for long ages past, but now revealed and made known through the prophetic writings by the command of the eternal God, so that all nations might believe and obey him— to the only wise God be glory forever through Jesus Christ! Amen. **Romans 16:25-27**

The gospel Paul was given to preach, although glorious and liberating, was one that challenged a lot of people who heard it. It not only challenged those outside the body of Christ but also many who were part of the body of Christ too. Paul was accused by many leaders within the church of the day as attempting to simply wipe way the Old Testament and the legal requirements attached to it. He was charged with creating his own idea of God's gospel by purposely ignoring the whole history of God in the Old Testament. Many claimed he was simply seeking to proclaim his own message, an *'easy believing message,'* at the expense of ignoring the Law and the Prophets.

Of course Paul didn't think this way at all. On the contrary, Paul embraced the Old Testament, not with a false understanding of it but as he saw God's true intentions within it. He never saw its true purpose as a written code describing how to obtain righteousness and blessings by works but rather he saw the message of Jesus within it and how, through Jesus, the glory prophesied in the Scriptures was now available for the church and established for us through the perfect redeeming work of Jesus. In fact, everything Paul preached can be found in the Old Testament.[16]

The Apostle Peter, at the time of writing his two letters to the church, also had this understanding when he looked into the Scriptures. He didn't see the prophets preaching rules and regulations; but rather, he saw that they were testifying to and prophesying about the coming of an era of grace for all.[17]

It seems apparent that Paul spent a great deal of time first looking into the Old Testament and finding the reality of Christ in the Scriptures and, through the Spirit making the mystery clear to him, writing to the church to share and make plain the amazing reality of Christ. He doesn't act like an academic and reference everything he was quoting or referring to; he just told it as he saw it. However, if you want to look you'll find the whole gospel message that Paul preached throughout the entire Old Testament and this is the point Paul makes in the introduction. He explains that this gospel he has spent his life

---

[16] They arranged to meet Paul on a certain day, and came in even larger numbers to the place where he was staying. From morning till evening he explained and declared to them the kingdom of God and tried to convince them about Jesus from the Law of Moses and from the Prophets. **Acts 28:23**

[17] Concerning this salvation, the prophets, who spoke of the grace that was to come to you, searched intently and with the greatest care, trying to find out the time and circumstances to which the Spirit of Christ in them was pointing when he predicted the sufferings of Christ and the glories that would follow. **1 Peter 1:10-11**

proclaiming was in fact promised beforehand through the prophets in the Holy Scriptures. He made the point that his message wasn't simply a new idea; rather, it was God's eternal idea coming to fulfilment.

That certainly is good news for us today because we can be assured that the gospel, that we are grounded and rejoice in, wasn't plan B or merely a new idea; but rather, it has always been the divine plan. It has always been God's eternal message to mankind yet it had been misunderstood and had been a mystery until the death and resurrection of Jesus. It is now, in the light of Christ, being made plain to all of mankind.

Paul was declaring that now through the power of the cross to establish it and through the grace God had poured out upon Paul to present it plainly; we, as the church, have entered into the eternal reality of God. Now as we look into the Scriptures, we see this reality. We see the grace of God, the spirit of Christ, and the story of Jesus everywhere.[18]

---

[18] He said to them, "This is what I told you while I was still with you: Everything must be fulfilled that is written about me in the Law of Moses, the Prophets and the Psalms." Then he opened their minds so they could understand the Scriptures. **Luke 24:44-45**

III

WHY TWO SAVIOURS IN SCRIPTURE?

The gospel God promised beforehand through his prophets in the Holy Scriptures regarding his Son, who as to his human nature was a descendant of David, and who through the Spirit of holiness was declared with power to be the Son of God by his resurrection from the dead: Jesus Christ our Lord. **Romans 1:2-5**

Paul makes the statement in his introductory remarks that within the Scriptures Jesus is testified to in two ways; according to his human nature and his divine nature. Jesus was fully God; however, in order to redeem mankind became fully human. This in and of itself is an amazing testimony of God's grace; that he would give up all that he was in the heavens and make himself like us on earth. It was in order to reveal just how gracious God is that Jesus became like us in our humanity so that through him we could become like him in his divinity.

Paul was helping his readers to understand how now, through the revelation of Christ, the Scriptures themselves found their fulfilment. Before the coming of Christ it remained a mystery as to just exactly who the Saviour would be. Would it be a man or would it be God himself? Scripture seemed to say both; however, without the revelation of Christ this had always been a striking contradiction.

Without the light of Christ it seemed to the reader of the Old Testament that there were two very different saviours. Sometimes God was talking about a servant[19] who was clearly an earthly man. He would be the one who would suffer for the sake of all the people and would be pierced for their transgressions. This earthly saviour was prophesied to be born through the line of David. There was clearly going to be this human saviour, he was going to be God's chosen man to save Israel, and be a light to the Gentiles as well. This was the testimony of the human saviour.

However, God also testified in other places within Scripture that there was no man, not even one, who was righteous and because there was no one capable of intervening to bring about salvation God himself[20] would intervene and save Israel. This was the testimony of the divine Saviour. So there seemed to be a continual pattern of two saviours prophesied in the Old Testament: one a man and the other God. It was a paradox that had no clear explanation and no apparent way to reconcile this obvious contradiction; that is, until the reality of Jesus was revealed to all mankind.

---

[19] **Isaiah 53**

[20] Truth is nowhere to be found, and whoever shuns evil becomes a prey. The LORD looked and was displeased that there was no justice. He saw that there was no one, he was appalled that there was no one to intervene; so his own arm worked salvation for him, and his own righteousness sustained him. **Isaiah 59:15-16**

It is through the cross and the revelation of Christ that we see this profound reality erupting in our hearts and filling us with joy as it reveals the heavenly revelation of God's salvation.[21] What no mind could have ever imagined was the very thing God had planned; that the two saviours, both the human and the divine, were actually the same Saviour who is our saviour Jesus Christ!

He was both the man, who, although equal with God, did not consider equality with God something to be grasped but humbled himself and came to earth to be born of a woman, to be born under the law to redeem those under law, as well as the perfect Son of God who was one with God, who is God, and has always been with God. He came down to earth so that he could fulfil the Scriptures that talked about the human saviour according to the line of David; however, He is also the divine Saviour, who, when no one else could be found, worked salvation on mankind's behalf.

So now we see in the Scriptures through the light of Christ, the reality of God's eternal salvation plan. As we now look back into the Holy Scriptures we can see the very person of Jesus all through the Old Testament. We can see the story of his grace; that he is, according to human nature, a descendent of David, and, through the spirit of holiness, the Son of God, one with God and the divine God himself. The revelation of how the human saviour and the divine Saviour can co-exist is revealed in the life of Jesus Christ. It is this reality that is testified to throughout the entire Old Testament.

As I stated earlier, the Apostle Paul was often charged with ignoring the Law and the Prophets in order to preach his version of the

---

[21] For God, who said, "Let light shine out of darkness," made his light shine in our hearts to give us the light of the knowledge of the glory of God in the face of Christ. **2 Corinthians 4:6**

gospel. Here, at the very beginning of his letter, he counters this charge as completely false stating in his introductory remarks that his whole gospel is preached through the Law and the Prophets not just in one or two places; but rather, all the way through it.

As we journey through the letter to the Romans, we will be walking with Paul as he takes the church on a journey all the way through the Scriptures in order to see the reality of Jesus. To Paul, everything in the Scriptures is there to testify about the life of Jesus. This is, in fact, the very same thing that Jesus said to the Pharisees in John's gospel:

You diligently study the Scriptures because you think that by them you possess eternal life. These are the Scriptures that testify about me, yet you refuse to come to me to have life. **John 5:39-40**

The truth is, if we want to understand the Scriptures and we want them to impart life to us we have to see Jesus in them. We, as the church, are now led by the Spirit and we are spiritual people. We operate and connect with God in the new way of the Spirit. God has given us the Spirit of his grace to empower us and work in us. It is for this reason that we can live a life that is obedient to God because Christ is living in us and for us; hence, we are no longer trying to do it all in our own strength by attempting to obey rules and regulations in the form of a written code.[22]

If we read the Scriptures looking for rules, tips, or guidelines for Godly living, then the Scriptures will have no value in terms of it

---

[22] I would like to learn just one thing from you: Did you receive the Spirit by observing the law, or by believing what you heard? Are you so foolish? After beginning with the Spirit, are you now trying to attain your goal by human effort? **Galatians 3:2-3**

imparting life to us; however, if we look into the Scriptures to see Jesus, his person, the story of his life, his sufferings, and the glories of his grace that came to us through his sufferings, then the Scriptures will joyfully impart life to us!

IV

CLARIFYING A MIXED MESSAGE

It's interesting to note that God actually told Paul at the start of his ministry that preaching the message of God's grace was going to be a tough task. Paul, however, gives us the impression he considered it a privilege to preach it regardless of the personal cost, regardless if people rejected the message, called it foolish, or went out of their way to discredit it. Paul still found that the greatest blessing in his life was the simple fact that we was given the honour to preach it, to live it, and to see the results of God's grace active in the lives of others who also accepted it.[23]

---

[23] We always thank God, the Father of our Lord Jesus Christ, when we pray for you, because we have heard of your faith in Christ Jesus and of the love you have for all the saints— the faith and love that spring from the hope that is stored up for you in heaven and that you have already heard about in the word of truth, the gospel that has come to you. All over the world this gospel is bearing fruit and growing, just as it has been doing among you since the day you heard it and understood God's grace in all its truth. **Colossians 1:3-6**

Paul's persecution did not come only from those outside the church. He had as many problems with people within the church as he did with those outside the church. Most likely he didn't get physically attacked by those inside the church although persecution and murder by the command of the leaders of the structured church against anyone who dared preach the same message Paul preached would become a common occurrence for close to two millennia. In Paul's day the violent opposition came mainly from religious institutional leaders who saw his message as a direct challenge to their own authority, power, and ability to make an income. As the church grew through the centuries, moving from an organic, relational community to a powerful religious institution, the violence that the religious institutions raged with against Paul was adopted by the very institution that claimed to be the gateway to the gospel. History, unfortunately, records the leadership of the organised church to have been one of the greatest persecutors to the gospel message; nevertheless, in Paul's day the seeds of opposition to the gospel message within the church community were already planted.[24]

In his other letters he recalled to the church how he was often treated like an imposter and a faker. He explained that although other preachers sought to discredit him by saying he wasn't competent to be an apostle, he rejoiced and replied that it was OK if he wasn't qualified in the eyes of other men because he knew that God credited him as competent. Paul lived out of a revelation that he was not competent because he was someone special or because other preachers

---

[24] Be shepherds of the church of God, which he bought with his own blood. I know that after I leave, savage wolves will come in among you and will not spare the flock. Even from your own number men will arise and distort the truth in order to draw away disciples after them. So be on your guard! Remember that for three years I never stopped warning each of you night and day with tears. **Acts 20:28-31**

commended him; but rather, because God made him competent to be a minister of the New Covenant by the working of his grace.[25]

Another major theme within Romans that Paul addresses is the reality of a life of obedience that comes from faith. Paul helped the church understand, and he is still helping us understand today, that our obedience to God does not come from the law; but rather, it comes from faith. That faith being in our new creation reality that we have received through the perfect work of Christ. It is living in this reality that produces obedience to God. It is a divine revelation and it is glorious; however, in order to accept and understand it we are first required to put aside our religious mindset and simply allow Paul to take us on a journey of understanding the good news of our new creation life and the empowerment of God that we have inherited in the gospel.

Most, if not all of us, have had religious tradition handed down to us and have been taught false, religiously minded ideas about the law in teaching that actually encourages us to embrace the law as a useful guide for good Christian living. What could be further from the truth? When these false beliefs regarding the law are left unchallenged or, even worse, actually encouraged, the result is what the apostle Paul refers to as spiritual slavery.[26]

The church in Galatia was actually greatly offended that Paul dared to stand up and challenge this mixed teaching. As I stated earlier, these other false teachers believed in Jesus, they believed he died on

---

[25] Not that we are competent in ourselves to claim anything for ourselves, but our competence comes from God. He has made us competent as ministers of a new covenant — not of the letter but of the Spirit; for the letter kills, but the Spirit gives life. **2 Corinthians 3:5-7**

[26] This matter arose because some false brothers had infiltrated our ranks to spy on the freedom we have in Christ Jesus and to make us slaves. We did not give in to them for a moment, so that the truth of the gospel might remain with you. **Galatians 2:4-5**

the cross for their sins, they believed he was raised again after three days, and they believed in the Holy Spirit; however, what they didn't believe was that Jesus had established a New Covenant of grace apart from law. Even if they found linguistic ways to still give lip service to the message of grace, they still found ways to mix in at least a few Old Testament laws that were beneficial to their ministry and theology. These other 'super apostles' preached grace but also law. They mixed them together because they simply could not understand how they could ever be separate. They loved the law and believed, falsely, that it was a moral guideline for righteous living and financial prosperity. When Paul corrected this false teaching so that the church would not become spiritually enslaved to a wrong theology, he was actually despised for it! He only wanted the church to be free in the truth of the gospel but the churches in Galatia actually took great offence at what Paul was saying; so much that they actually started thinking of him as their enemy! Paul had to ask them:

Have I now become your enemy by telling you the truth? Those people are zealous to win you over, but for no good. What they want is to alienate you from us, so that you may have zeal for them.
Galatians 4:16-17

Just like the early church Paul originally wrote to, when we are challenged with the possibility that we have believed the wrong thing about the law we can easily become offended, find ourselves trying to defend the law, and defend the teachers or leaders who have convinced us we should be zealous for the law. This does us no favours; in fact, we only find ourselves defending a theology of slavery while rejecting the freedom Christ died to establish for us.

There comes a point in all our lives where we have to acknowledge that we have thought of the law, to some degree, in the wrong way. Paul himself had to accept he had been terribly wrong about God's law and God's way on the road to Damascus. He had spent his entire life zealous for the law as a means of works based righteousness. On the road to Damascus he too had to listen to the voice of the Spirit, humble himself, and allow his understanding of the law and its purpose to fall into line with the reality of Jesus.

It was Jesus who gave Paul the grace to explain this glorious revelation. Paul was called for such a task and was given the revelation directly into his spirit in order that at least one person could grasp what simply does not come natural to the religious mind. Paul was called by Jesus as the 'instrument' through which the church could hear and comprehend the reality of God's eternal plan. In fact, although the other apostles had walked with Jesus spending every day with him, they too misunderstood Jesus and the reality of a New Covenant of grace apart from law.

It was Paul who brought this reality to the centre stage of the church community so that the other apostles and leaders could finally grasp the reality of the gospel of God's grace through Paul. If we are willing to open our hearts to hear what Paul has to say and what the Spirit has to say through Paul's letter I believe we will be greatly blessed. We too can be liberated in the good news and experience a greater freedom in our spirits. It is, after all, for freedom that Jesus came and it is for freedom that Jesus set us free. So then, let's understand how to be truly free; free from sin, free from the wrong understanding of the law, and free to live an empowered life unto God.

V

HOW TO BE A SAINT

To all in Rome who are loved by God and called to be saints: Grace and peace to you from God our Father and from the Lord Jesus Christ.
Romans 1:7

Paul makes the statement in his opening remarks that the church in Rome was indeed a church community that was loved by God and called to be saints. This is, in essence, really the initial experience that happens to all of us when we first unite ourselves with Jesus. We experience this new reality where the Spirit indwells us and reveals this newly created spiritual understanding: *"I am loved by God."*

In Christ, God also calls us saints because everyone who is in Christ is a saint. God not only calls us saints but he also encourages us that we will outlive the life of a saint. A saint in Christ is not defined in the same manner as the world defines a saint. A saint in the world is someone who excludes themselves from anything they deem to be unholy or indulgent. God's definition of a saint has nothing to do with what one excludes themselves from; rather, it has everything to do with whom they have been included in.

A saint to God is simply someone who is in Christ and allows Christ to live his life through them. We are now saints because we have accepted God's invitation into the good news and now allow Christ to live his life through us. Not only that, but we also receive the blessedness to actively partake in that life with Christ because we are one with Jesus. It's not that Christ now lives in us and we have no active part; not at all, we are very much an active part; however, we realise that the power is coming from Christ in us.

The truth is that when we united ourselves with Jesus we became one with him in his death;[27] therefore, we now remain united with him in his resurrection. We are now walking and living this life united with Christ. We walk with a revelation that we are one with Jesus and that is why God calls us saints. We are saints of grace. The true sign of a saint is the natural overflow of grace for others *because that is the very heart and nature of God himself.* We benefit from a grace empowered life that shines God's nature of love and we can rest knowing that it's not our power that outworks this life; rather, it is Christ's power.[28] It is Christ in us who lives and that is why we are assured that as we walk we are walking in a way that is pleasing to God.

Jesus came to give us rest. He gives us the blessedness of resting in God's presence without fear that we will be judged or condemned for our weaknesses or failings. In Christ, his perfect

---

[27] Now if we died with Christ, we believe that we will also live with him. **Romans 6:8**

[28] We proclaim him, admonishing and teaching everyone with all wisdom, so that we may present everyone perfect in Christ. To this end I labor, struggling with all his energy, which so powerfully works in me. **Colossians 1:28-29**

sacrifice upon the cross was enough to completely cleanse us and make us holy and acceptable to God. It is this wonderful rest that we receive through the grace of Jesus that empowers us to truly live in the obedience and the good news of God. When we don't cling to religious ideas and religious traditions that we have been taught and indoctrinated into; but rather, lay them aside and open our hearts by listening to what Paul has to say to us regarding our inheritance and new creation life in Christ, then we too can be greatly encouraged and find ourselves truly rested in our faith and relationship with God.

It's also interesting to note that the first statement Paul makes to the Roman church after his brief introduction is the same statement he makes to all the churches he wrote to and that is that *'God's grace and peace'* is for the church. It seems Paul lived out of a revelation that, as a preacher and a leader in God's community, he needed to continually establish the church in their inheritance; that inheritance being, that God's grace and God's peace was for them.

It does not matter how far wrong you may have gone, God's grace is for your life. If you are in Christ, the old has gone, the new has come, and all of this is to the glory of God.[29] When we rest in this reality it gives us the empowerment to actually live in a way that is pleasing to God which is living with a revelation of the Christ who is in you and letting that grace flow out of you. It is through living with the revelation of the 'Christ in us' that empowers us to not be judgemental towards others because of their weakness; rather, we can be full of grace towards them. We can have grace for them in their weaknesses just as God always has grace for us; and, just as grace

---

[29] So from now on we regard no one from a worldly point of view. Though we once regarded Christ in this way, we do so no longer. Therefore, if anyone is in Christ, he is a new creation; the old has gone, the new has come! **2 Corinthians 5:16-17**

transformed our lives, that same grace now working through us can be used to transform the lives of others, too.

VI

How Paul Shared the Message of Grace

Paul thanked God for the Roman church. He also purposely commented on the fact that their church was known around the world for their faith. They were evidently a passionate church; however, they were clearly still lacking the foundational understanding of living in the grace of God apart from law. In addressing this issue it's worth taking note that Paul didn't act anywhere near as harshly to them as he did to the churches in Galatia. It is clear that the Roman church misunderstood the fullness of the gospel but Paul took a very different approach with them than he did with the Galatian church. When Paul talked to the Galatians he was much more emotional and he seemed to take their rejection of his gospel much more personally. He was shocked how they had turned from the gospel foundation that he had preached to them, established them in, and had turned to another gospel.

The difference between the two churches was that Paul never laid the foundation in Rome. He never taught them the foundational teaching of the good news of God's grace apart from law, and, because of this, Paul didn't rebuke the church for believing a 'different' gospel as he did with the Galatians.

I believe this is an important point to consider for preachers today. We cannot be overly critical of other church communities that don't understand the reality of God's grace apart from law if they have never been taught it to begin with. If we have not been personally involved in laying the foundation of the gospel in their community then we cannot take offence at their lack of understanding; but rather, we can offer our gift as communicators of God's grace to build the church up and help them see the greater reality of the gospel that is rightly theirs in Christ.

If it is in our own church communities, the ones that we have been personally involved in preaching the foundational truths in and we know that they had clearly understood and embraced it but then consciously turned away from it to embrace another gospel, then that may be a situation to be somewhat stronger in our approach and correction. However, if it is another local church community, one that we have not laid the foundations in, then we need to encourage them through love and serve them with a spirit of love and grace to help them embrace the greater reality that is rightly theirs in Christ.

Paul wanted to first acknowledge that the Roman church's faith had a great reputation but he also wanted to take them on a journey. Although the church was full of faith and loved Christ, many still couldn't grasp how it is possible that they can now be in a New Covenant that is completely apart from the law. That, I believe, was their greatest difficulty and the foundational reason Paul wrote to them in the first place.

As we discussed earlier, Paul evidently had some personal relationships with some of the leaders within the Roman church community. It was one of these friends who most likely had contacted Paul and explained that many in the church were still clinging to the idea that the law is the means to become righteous and that it was the law instead of Christ in them that caused them to have knowledge and the ability to understand truth. Before Paul jumped into talking about this very topic, he first expressed his heart to the church. He wanted the church to know that he loved them and that he cared deeply for them. Paul explained to them how he not only served God with all his heart but he was also constantly thinking about the church in Rome, praying for them, and explaining to them that one of his heart's desires was that God would make the way possible for him to visit them. Paul lived from the reality of love, which is the highest form of truth:

*If I have the gift of prophecy and can fathom all mysteries and all knowledge, and if I have a faith that can move mountains, but do not have love, I am nothing. **1 Corinthians 13:2***

I believe this, above all else, is the heart behind Paul's message and ministry. It's the way all of us who call ourselves ministers of the good news of God's grace should be led. I'm sure you would agree: *Love is the way.* Love is what opens up the hearts of our listeners to hear and accept what we have to share.

VII

WHY PAUL WAS UNASHAMED OF THE GOSPEL

Paul was passionate about preaching the gospel and helping people get established in the reality of Christ. It was what drove him, going so far as to explain that he felt obligated to everyone; whoever was willing to listen to him declare the good news. This was the very thing he desired to do in Rome. Towards the climax of his introduction he also makes a fascinating statement regarding the gospel he had spent his life preaching. He said:

I am not ashamed of the gospel, because it is the power of God for the salvation of everyone who believes: first or the Jew, then for the Gentile. **Romans 1:16**

It is an incredible statement he made when you consider that this letter to the Romans was written after a life time of ministry that included the very public Corinthian debaucheries and the Galatians'

47

rejection of Paul and his gospel. He went through his whole life preaching Christ and the good news of the New Covenant reality: the good news of God's grace apart from law. He continually served people, humbling himself and serving communities where they were at in the hope that they would take hold of this wonderful reality.[30] Paul was not standing proud and pressuring people to accept his theology. To Paul the gospel was a reality and not a theory and something he outlived in his life as well as his preaching.

It was well documented that other preachers felt it their duty to slander the ministry of Paul, having the intention of exposing him as an illegitimate apostle, and his message not worth trusting in. If they needed proof, they only needed to point to the church communities he founded and highlight the terrible mess they were all in. Perhaps they went about publicly slandering and humiliating Paul with the hope of pressuring him to change his message to include not only the finished work of Jesus but also the unfinished work of the law. It seems that their slander was an attempt to expose his message as faulty making the charge that he and his churches were wrong. They believed he should have been preaching the law to the churches he founded. He should have told them that they were sinners and they needed to clean up their act. He should have hit them with the law; instead, Paul reached out with grace.

Paul never buckled to such preachers; rather, his attitude was focused on the work of Christ and he was steadfast in his believe that if anyone had accepted Christ then they were a new creation, the old had gone and the new had come, and all this was to the glory of God. Paul

---

[30] To the weak I became weak, to win the weak. I have become all things to all men so that by all possible means I might save some. **1 Corinthians 9:22**

refused to preach to the believer's *'old self.'* He maintained that the old self died with Christ in his death and every believer had been raised with Christ in his resurrection and made a new creation. In Christ we are all new. Paul was committed to maintaining this was indeed every Christian's reality and that was the perspective he preached from. He was steadfast in his belief that the new man could not be broken like the old man and believing that Christ in the believer was strong enough to walk out the 'God life' in their life. They only needed to put their confidence in him and in the reality that was rightly theirs in him. What broke the old man could not break the new man. The need for the believer wasn't to hear about their old self but to hear of the reality of their new self and be given the confidence to live in it.

Paul's ministry was constantly being discredited. Some simply dismissed him as a fool, some took offence at him, and others slandered him as a false teacher. Everything that he did was continually slandered and yet even at the point of writing his letter to the Romans, even after all the setbacks, the failures, and the misunderstandings that took place in the churches he founded he still was preaching the good news of God's grace apart from law.

It was after all this that he wrote within his letter to the Romans this bold statement that *he was not ashamed of the gospel*, because Paul knew it was the reality of God. Paul didn't care how discredited he got and how many people called him a fool by pointing out his failings, how he wasn't a trained speaker, and how he often stumbled upon his words.[31] Paul maintained he was not ashamed because, despite his lack, weakness, and failings, the gospel message

---

[31] But I do not think I am in the least inferior to those "super-apostles." I may not be a trained speaker, but I do have knowledge. We have made this perfectly clear to you in every way.
2 Corinthians 11:5-6

he preached was, nonetheless, the power of God! He wasn't ashamed of the gospel and today we too join Paul as a community of people who are not ashamed of the gospel because the gospel of God's grace apart from law is the power of God. It is the power of God for our obedience, righteousness, holiness, wisdom, and salvation. Whatever you need to be saved from, this gospel is the power that brings that salvation into your life.

It is the gospel that lifts up Jesus, boasts in the glory of who he is, and in the incomparable riches of his grace. It is the message that rejoices in Jesus, in his glory, in his power, and in his person. It is the good news that reveals his finished work proclaiming that Jesus was powerful enough to fulfil the Old Covenant and powerful enough to establish the New Covenant.[32] It is the message that testifies to the truth that his sacrifice on the cross and the spilling of his blood was powerful enough to cleanse us perfectly. It is the good news that declares that Jesus is powerful enough to make us new, perfect, and whole in him.[33]

Paul was preaching the same message his whole life which is the message of the gospel that is truly glorious and gives all credit to God and when believed upon causes the 'Christ life' to be lived out victoriously in the life of all who believe. Paul didn't look to his own ministry's fruit or what other people were saying to decide what truth was; rather, he looked to the gospel that God gave him and knew that it was the truth and that was his reason for preaching it.

---

[32] When you were dead in your sins and in the uncircumcision of your sinful nature, God made you alive with Christ. He forgave us all our sins, having cancelled the written code, with its regulations, that was against us and that stood opposed to us; he took it away, nailing it to the cross. **Colossians 2:13-14**

[33] Because by one sacrifice he has made perfect forever those who are being made holy. **Hebrews 10:14**

It is in this gospel that Paul proclaimed, a righteousness from God is revealed; a righteousness by faith. Paul is leading up to explaining to the church how righteousness is not revealed *in the law*; but rather, *in the gospel*: the good news of God's grace.

Most of the church members in Rome were still holding onto their religious, traditional mindset that the law was God's revelation of righteousness to mankind but now Paul was walking them through the understanding of God's true definition of righteousness. It is a journey that not only the Roman church needed to take but all of us need to walk through in order to truly become comfortable with this profound and glorious reality. Righteousness is, in fact, not an action but a person – and he is living in you: Christ in you, your hope of glory!

It is because of him that you are in Christ Jesus, who has become for us wisdom from God—that is, our righteousness, holiness and redemption. **1 Corinthians 1:30**

VIII

The Mystery Revealed

For in the gospel a righteousness from God is revealed, a righteousness that is by faith from first to last, just as it is written: "The righteous will live by faith." **Romans 1:17**

When Paul made this bold statement that now after the death and resurrection of Jesus a righteousness from God had been revealed, he didn't mean that it was revealed through his ideas or thoughts. Paul didn't make the gospel up! He received a divine revelation of Christ and it was through this revelation of the ultimate supremacy of Christ that he was enabled to finally see the truth in the Scriptures – for now he could see Jesus. To Paul's amazement, he realised he could actually find the testimony of the life and accomplishments of Jesus in every Scripture. The good news of God's grace, the New Covenant, and righteousness by faith had always been testified to; however, without the revelation of the supremacy of Jesus and what his death and resurrection accomplished for us, it had always remained a mystery. As Paul said in his letter to the Corinthians:

Therefore, since we have such a hope, we are very bold. We are not like Moses, who would put a veil over his face to keep the Israelites from gazing at it while the radiance was fading away. But their minds were made dull, for to this day the same veil remains when the old covenant is read. It has not been removed, because only in Christ is it taken away. Even to this day when Moses is read, a veil covers their hearts. But whenever anyone turns to the Lord, the veil is taken away.
2 Corinthians 3:12-16

Without the light of Christ we all continue to read the Old Testament as if it were veiled of its true meaning and intention; however, now that we are in Christ that veil has been removed and we can clearly see the story of Jesus and the message of God's righteousness that is given as a gift that is not earned by our own obedience to a written code; rather, it is a righteousness that is given through our acceptance of God's Son.

When Paul made this bold statement about righteousness by faith he backed up his statement by quoting a Scripture from the Old Testament because when Paul looked at the Old Testament he saw the story of Jesus all through it. Jesus himself helped two of his disciples understand this Scriptural reality as he walked along the road to Emmaus with them. Luke records how Jesus opened up their eyes to see him in all the Scriptures starting with Moses and going through all the prophets.[34]

The whole Bible testifies about Jesus and the grace that comes to us through him. The Scriptures were never given to help mankind understand how to live *before God;* rather, they were given to reveal and testify to the life story of Jesus, his suffering, and the grace which would be given to us through his resurrection in order that we would come to understand that we have been granted the blessing of being able to live *in God.*[35]

How wonderful to know that God's intention for the Bible was not to give us a rule book or a life-application-manual; rather, his desire was to give us a testimony of the Life in us: that is Christ in us, our hope of glory! Now if the testimony is true, and Christ did in fact do everything the Bible testifies to, then we can rest assured that God's righteousness that comes by faith is already radically alive and active in us. We can rest in the truth of God's good news and be assured that God is working powerfully in and through us at the same time.[36]

---

[34] He said to them, "How foolish you are, and how slow of heart to believe all that the prophets have spoken! Did not the Christ have to suffer these things and then enter his glory?" And beginning with Moses and all the Prophets, he explained to them what was said in all the Scriptures concerning himself. **Luke 24:25-27**

[35] Set your minds on things above, not on earthly things. 3 For you died, and your life is now hidden with Christ in God. **Colossians 3:2-3**

[36] All over the world this gospel is bearing fruit and growing, just as it has been doing among you since the day you heard it and understood God's grace in all its truth. **Philippians 1:6**

IV

WHY DID PAUL TALK ABOUT
UNRIGHTEOUSNESS?

Paul made his big, bold statement about a righteousness that comes by faith, knowing it would spark his reader's curiosity, and then unexpectedly changed the topic to expound on unrighteousness. It is somewhat striking to witness Paul suddenly changing direction within his letter, from a righteousness by faith to a dialogue about unrighteousness. At this point in reading the letter we really must ask ourselves the question: 'Why did Paul do such a thing?'

I believe Paul did this because he knew that before the church could understand God's divine reality of 'righteousness as a gift,' they first needed to also be clear that righteousness could not be obtained by any other means. Up until this point, many in the church still believed that righteousness could be obtained through works; that is, through obedience to the law. It is this error in thinking that Paul wanted to expose in order that the church could be liberated from this false understanding and truly embrace the truth about righteousness. It is for this reason that Paul switched topics, momentarily, in his letter and began to expound on *unrighteousness.*

Paul, always two steps ahead in his thinking, was creating the opportunity to expose and highlight this false understanding of the law that many in the Roman church still held strongly to in order to explain the correct perspective of righteousness in the following chapters as well as giving a clearly defined understanding of the law throughout the rest of his letter.

The Roman church had a mixture of people from different backgrounds. Many came from a Jewish background and these members were still holding to the traditional teachings about the Scriptures they were taught in their childhood. They had grown up being taught that the Law of Moses was God's guideline to becoming a righteous person; moreover, a rulebook that any God fearing person could diligently follow in order to obtain a status of righteousness. These Jewish Christians had come to accept Jesus as the Christ which changed the way they understood God a great deal; however, that didn't change the way they viewed the law. They still believed that the Law of Moses was naturally the key to righteousness. This led to the assumption that the pagans around them, who didn't have God's law, were naturally unrighteous.

Paul purposely wrote this opening section regarding unrighteousness in such a way that, at first glance it would seem apparent that he was addressing the Gentile world. It's true that he was, at least in part, but Paul was doing much more than just that. He was actually setting the stage to highlight the parallels between the Gentile world, who, without God's written law to guide them, were unrighteous, and Israel, who, although they had a covenant of God's written law, were equally unrighteous.

This parallel is strikingly obvious in Scripture once we are made aware of it but many in the Roman church needed Paul's unique insight to see this. Paul's ultimate goal in this section of his letter was not to highlight the problem of unrighteousness; but rather, *to highlight the problem of being judgemental.*

It was common in the early church as it has been throughout church history, to misuse God's written word in order to point the finger and condemn others. This misuse of God's written law was also used by the Pharisees in the days of Jesus who looked down their nose at the people and nations around them with bitter judgement in their hearts and eyes, while, at the same time, being blind to the plank in their own eyes. Although they could see that those without God's written law were unrighteous, they failed to see that they too, who had the written law, were just as unrighteous and doing all the same unrighteous activities.

When we look to the testimony of Israel's history alongside the history of the nations around them, we find that they actually shared the same unrighteous story. Paul's intention was to show the church that if the law had been powerless to make Israel righteous then why did they believe it was the answer to making the Gentile world or the church righteous? Paul was highlighting in this section of his letter that Israel, although they had the law, were still as unrighteous as those who didn't have the law. He wanted to show the church that the law never helped those who were under the law to be righteous, because, in fact, that was never the law's ministry to begin with.

We need to understand this reality so that we don't defend the law as a written code that delivers a righteous status before God. When we think of the law as a tool that can be used to force an ungodly world, as well as the church community, to live a righteous life we set ourselves up for disaster.

Paul revealed that if the law which was used as a written code throughout the Old Covenant didn't succeed in making anyone righteous, not even one, then we can be sure it won't make anyone righteous now, or ever. We now live and relate with God in the new way of the Spirit of grace and not in the old way of the written code of law. It is through this new and living way that we can be righteous: not by law, but by faith in the one who fulfilled the law upon the cross.

It is of the upmost importance for us to understand the purpose Paul had in writing about 'unrighteousness' in the opening chapter of his letter, how it has been used to cause so much damage by religiously minded Christians who have taken this part of Paul's letter and used it *out of context* to condemn and judge people in the world. That is such a terrible tragedy. Indeed, this small section of Paul's letter has been used as a platform to judge and condemn people for centuries. That was never Paul's intention for writing it; in fact, Paul's intention was the complete opposite!

Paul's true intention was to make clear to the members of the church that they had no right to judge anyone. Rather than being judgemental, their focus should have been on living their lives out of a position of grace. This section of the letter was written, as a forerunner of sorts, to make it all the clearer how much God loves us, that he would send his Son to die for us, even when we were so ungodly! Paul talks about all the ungodliness in the world to firstly highlight the fact that those who were under the law were also doing the same ungodly things, and, even more amazingly, that regardless of all the terrible sins that were committed, whether by Jew or Gentile, God's love for mankind was bigger than all of them and he had made a way to freely justify all by his grace.[37]

It is a divine revelation to understand that God isn't actually trying to force people to change their sinful ways; rather, he desires that they would look at the love he has for them pictured in the cross of Christ. He knows that when they get a revelation of his love for them, they will come to him and be changed by his grace forever. We do God a disservice when we tell the world God is condemning them for their sins. Jesus himself declared to all of us that God didn't send him into the world to condemn it, but to save it through him.[38]

God doesn't ask people to change, and he doesn't stand in judgement for their sins: God sent his Son to die for those people while they were in those sins! The reality Paul was presenting to the church showed a God of all grace who doesn't treat sinners with judgement, although he could; rather, he treated them with the fullness of his grace, going so far as to pay the full penalty for their sins before they even believed: a grace towards mankind that was fulfilled in the cross of Jesus.

Some members of the Roman church thought it was still acceptable to judge the Gentiles around them, and perhaps even other

---

[37] You see, at just the right time, when we were still powerless, Christ died for the ungodly. Very rarely will anyone die for a righteous man, though for a good man someone might possibly dare to die. But God demonstrates his own love for us in this: While we were still sinners, Christ died for us. **Romans 5:6-8**

[38] For God so loved the world that he gave his one and only Son, that whoever believes in him shall not perish but have eternal life. For God did not send his Son into the world to condemn the world, but to save the world through him. **John 3:16-17**

members of the church, as unrighteous. Their way of justifying such actions was by pointing to the written words of God found in the Bible. Paul revealed, through this letter, how this was not only a theologically wrong position, but it would also evoke a personal, downward spiral into sin for anyone who stubbornly persisted to use the Bible in such a way.

The reason for this is because the written word of God in its correct usage is a testimony to the person of Jesus. Quoting verses from the Bible as a way to judge others or pressure them to submit to some kind of moral or ethical viewpoint cannot impart life; however, you can use the Bible effectively to point to the one who gives his righteousness, along with the ability to live morally and ethically, away freely as a gift. Jesus is the reality of God's voice to mankind: his Word now revealed. The written code is of great value if it is seen as a John the Baptist type figure. John had a powerful ministry in that he was sent ahead of Jesus to prepare the way for him. We can be very thankful that John came before Jesus to testify of him and prepare the way for him; however, we would be very foolish and very wrong to think that John the Baptist is God's eternal prophet we are still required to follow. *To think of the law as a possible way of man obtaining righteousness is like following John the Baptist believing him to be the Christ.* Both the law and John the Baptist had very valuable and wonderful ministries; however, when we think of them in the wrong way we can find ourselves with very destructive theology.

It was easy for the church in Rome to look at the Gentile world and assume the reason for their unrighteousness was due to the fact they didn't have the Law of Moses as a guide to right living; Paul was pointing out that this was in fact a false belief to have. The reason he was exposing this was because Paul wanted the church to come to an understanding that there had to be something else besides the law which made people righteous. Clearly the law did not make those who were under it righteous for they too fell short of the glory of God just like the Gentiles around them who didn't have the law.

Paul's short discourse on unrighteousness has a much larger setting that can be found throughout the rest of the Old Testament Scriptures. When we look back into Scripture we can begin to see the parallels that Paul was making between Israel and the Gentile world. We read how the history of Israel reveals their complete failure to live up to any standards of righteousness according to the written code, highlighting the fact that the law, which was used purely as a written rulebook to follow, doesn't make anyone righteous. Without this understanding it is easy to use the law incorrectly as a tool to judge oneself and also others. Some members of the church believed that they had a right to judge people based on what was written in the Bible; however, Paul was showing that no one had the right to use the written code to judge anyone because those under the mentality of using the Bible as a legal document about rules and requirements were in fact just as guilty of breaking the rules they were barking at others.

That's why God gave us the New Covenant - apart from law, so that he could impart his righteousness through Christ to all as a gift and if it is a gift then none of us can turn around and judge others for being unrighteous. Instead, we joyfully point out the one who gave us his righteousness. We don't live under the law but rather we live under grace.[39] What a blessing that God now allows us to live under his

---

[39] For sin shall not be your master, because you are not under law, but under grace.
Romans 6:4

divine nature, that is his grace, so that we can impart grace to people who are weak by not judging them; rather, we can reveal the nature of God to them. Living in the new way of the Spirit means that we are wonderfully empowered by grace to live in obedience to God and we can shine his love and grace into the world around us. It is beneficial and also the very foundation of our faith, to live in God's grace and embrace it.

God's power comes directly through his grace. Obedience requires power from heaven and that empowerment is given through God's grace in our lives. That is why now we can be obedient by faith because through our faith we have received an abundance of grace and that grace is the power in our life to walk in God's ways. The truth is that the Bible, when used as a moral guideline, is totally powerless and useless. It is important for all of us to understand and accept that it is not the *written word of God* on stone and paper which is our hope of glory; rather, it is the *living word of God* in us, Christ in us, who is our hope of glory.[40]

"For what the Law was powerless to do, in that it was weakened by the sinful nature, God did by sending his own Son in the likeness of sinful man, and condemned sin." **Romans 8:3**

---

[40] To them God has chosen to make known among the Gentiles the glorious riches of this mystery, which is Christ in you, the hope of glory. **Colossians 1:27**

X

THE JEWISH AND GENTILE PARALLELS

Paul's main motive in his discourse about unrighteousness in his opening statements in his letter was ultimately to help the church in Rome see the parallels between the Israel and Gentile worlds and how they had more in common than perhaps initially believed. It was easy for those with a Jewish background to enjoy the belief that their nation was indeed the most righteous nation on earth because of the unique benefit of having God's law as their guide. At the same time, it must have been quite a sobering revelation to see that actually, just as the Scriptures clearly testified and portrayed, their nation was in fact equally as unrighteous as all the other nations of the world. It is with this in mind, we now take a closer look at some of these parallels relating to this particular part of Paul's dialogue found in the Scriptures. Paul starts by stating that:

The wrath of God is being revealed from heaven against all the godlessness and wickedness of men who suppress the truth by their wickedness. **Romans 1:18**

Although this was true for the Gentile world who didn't have the law, Paul's purpose for making this particular point was to highlight to the Jewish Christians in Rome the parallels to Israel's history. As Moses testified in the book of Deuteronomy, Israel, who was under the law, was just as guilty of suppressing the truth of God by their wickedness.

Remember your servants Abraham, Isaac and Jacob. Overlook the stubbornness of this people, their wickedness and their sin. **Deuteronomy 9:27**

Paul continued in his letter to explaining that:

What may be known about God was plain to the pagan world, because God has made it plain to them and therefore they were without excuse. **Romans 1:19**

These comments from Paul highlighted the point that if the pagans were without excuse for their wickedness, how much more should Israel be without excuse? God made his ways even plainer to them and yet they were, like the pagan world, nonetheless disobedient.

If you obey the LORD your God and keep his commands and decrees that are written in this Book of the Law and turn to the LORD your God with all your heart and with all your soul. Now what I am commanding you today is not too difficult for you or beyond your reach. **Deuteronomy 30:10-11**

Paul continued to point out the godlessness of the Gentile world and how:

For although they knew God, they neither glorified him as God nor gave thanks to him, but their thinking became futile and their foolish hearts were darkened. **Romans 1:21**

He points out that:

Although they claimed to be wise, they became fools and exchanged the glory of the immortal God for images made to look like mortal man and birds and animals and reptiles. **Romans 1:22-23**

Paul is once more detailing this to help the church identify that these were extremely unrighteous acts and also to realise that the very people who had the law were also doing these unrighteous acts as well. In fact, Israel had just been given the law when they indulged in these very behaviours. The words of the law would have still been fresh in their thoughts during the very time when they exchanged the glory of the immortal God for the image of a golden calf!

Then the LORD said to Moses, "Tell the Israelites this: 'You have seen for yourselves that I have spoken to you from heaven: Do not make any gods to be alongside me; do not make for yourselves gods of silver or gods of gold. **Exodus 20:22**

*When Moses went and told the people all the LORD's words and laws, they responded with one voice, "Everything the LORD has said we will do." **Exodus 24:3***

*When the people saw that Moses was so long in coming down from the mountain, they gathered around Aaron and said, "Come, make us gods who will go before us. As for this fellow Moses who brought us up out of Egypt, we don't know what has happened to him." Aaron answered them, "Take off the gold earrings that your wives, your sons and your daughters are wearing, and bring them to me." So all the people took off their earrings and brought them to Aaron. He took what they handed him and made it into an idol cast in the shape of a calf, fashioning it with a tool. Then they said, "These are your gods, O Israel, who brought you up out of Egypt." **Exodus 32:1-4***

God is the God of all grace who saved Israel from slavery completely based on his love towards them, and what did Israel do? They exchanged the truth of God for a lie, going so far as to give a golden calf, the work of their hands, the credit for bringing them out of Egypt.

How could Aaron give credit to a golden calf for the redeeming work that the glorious, almighty God did? And yet that is what he did. That is what the entire community embraced and desired.

This was just after the point that they were given the law. If the law imparted or helped people to be righteous it would have surely produced righteous results at this time. They should have been more holy than ever if the law imparted righteousness and yet it actually seemed to have caused the opposite result: it caused their sinful activity to increase.

Paul was showing the church through making these parallels that it is easy to cast judgement against the world based on the law; however, the law didn't help the Israelites to be righteous even though they had it. In fact, it only caused them to become even more unrighteous. When we as the church understand this, we won't use the Bible to judge and condemn others; instead, we will be people of grace, people who don't cast a finger at others because they are sinners; but rather, have hearts full of grace for people and allow the Spirit of love to pour out of us.

It's easy to look at the world with judgement and condemn them as being idol worshippers who worship money, fame, and other 'sinful' things while justifying our judgemental actions by quoting God's Scriptures. The problem with this is that to use the Scriptures to condemn others one has to only use them as a written code *and exclude the Spirit of Christ within them.* Jesus is the living word of God; active and full of grace. To use the Scriptures in line with God's truth, we have to apply them in the light of Christ and the gift of his grace.

Paul showed that the law can never be used to cast judgement on the unrighteous because those who were given it by God were not righteously transformed by it. Instead of lifting up the law and trying to condemn people into righteousness, we should be simply lifting up the reality of Christ and the wonder of his love and grace. The law won't make the sinner in the world righteous because the law didn't make anyone righteous. Instead, we should be presenting the good news of God's grace, the Spirit of Christ, and the power of his finished work because that is God's power unto salvation.

Paul continued to highlight the parallels in the history of both the Jew and Gentile, how they equally fell short of the glory of God, and dived head first into the same sinful works. Next, Paul brings up the issue of sexual impurity, the degrading of their bodies with one another, and talking again about the same people who exchanged the glory of God for an image made to look like animals and reptiles. Paul was referring to both Israel as well as the pagan nations around them. Paul explained how:

In the same way the men abandoned natural relations with women and were inflamed with lust for one another and how men committed indecent acts with other men. **Romans 1:26**

Not only was Paul addressing the sexual impurity of those in the world who did not have a covenant with God nor his written law to follow, but most likely he was also making reference to the tribe of Benjamin who were Israelites who had the law but were; nonetheless, sexually immoral and indulging in some of the most degrading acts recorded in Scripture.

While they were enjoying themselves, some of the wicked men of the city surrounded the house. Pounding on the door, they shouted to the old man who owned the house, "Bring out the man who came to your *house so we can have sex with him." **Judges 19:22***

Paul knew that the church would have initially only seen the pagans and the unbelievers in the world as sexually immoral. What Paul also wanted the church to recognise is that even men from the tribe of Benjamin, who had the law and were under the law, were sexually immoral. Yes, it may very well be true that the pagans are unrighteous and involved in sexual sins but so too were those who were under the law. Once again we see Paul highlighting to the church that the law was not in any way a means to bring about a righteous life. Those without it were unrighteous but so too were those under it.

Paul continues on with his dialogue about the Gentile world's unrighteousness and paralleling it to Israel's unrighteousness. He was pushing the point that the Gentile world was apart from God's written law had clearly fallen short of God's glory, but so too, did Israel who had God's written law. Although they had been given the law by God himself, they were in fact guilty of all of the same unrighteous acts as the Gentiles were. The Scriptures testify to us that the law did not help them in any way be righteous. This was not Paul's opinion; however, he was simply pointing out God's own testimony of their disobedience from the Scriptures:

Remember this and never forget how you provoked the LORD your *God to anger in the desert. From the day you left Egypt until you* *arrived here, you have been rebellious against the LORD.* ***Deuteronomy 9:7***

And the LORD told him: "Listen to all that the people are saying to you; it is not you they have rejected, but they have rejected me as their king. As they have done from the day I brought them up out of Egypt until this day, forsaking me and serving other gods, so they are doing to you. **1 Samuel 7-8**

From the time your forefathers left Egypt until now, day after day, again and again I sent you my servants the prophets. But they did not listen to me or pay attention. They were stiff-necked and did more evil than their forefathers.' **Jeremiah 7:25-26**

"Therefore this is what the Sovereign LORD says: You have been more unruly than the nations around you and have not followed my decrees or kept my laws. You have not even conformed to the standards of the nations around you. **Ezekiel 5:7**

It is important to remember that God still moved by his grace amongst his people in the Old Testament; however, we also must recognise that the people, left to their own efforts, were purposely recorded as being consistently disobedient. Paul finishes his short dialogue on unrighteousness and brings his readers to a point of understanding that although it is clear that the Gentile world was living an ungodly lifestyle, so too had the Israelites lived an ungodly lifestyle. The Gentiles didn't have the law and the Jews did; however, the end result was no different. Both Jew and Gentile fell short of the glory of God. That clearly meant that having and attempting to follow the law as a written instruction manual was not the deciding factor on whether someone would live a righteous life or not. In fact, it made the point all the more clearer that the law as a written code that man could quote to judge others was not in any way useful for bringing about a righteous life.

Paul's point was that we as the church cannot think the written law of God is the answer to stopping mankind or fellow members of the church from living an unrighteous lifestyle. Although it's true that people are actively sinning in the world, trying to enforce the written code of God upon them will not accomplish anything because God's word, in the form of a written code, will never impart righteousness. The truth is it will only push them further into sin. What we need to actually do is give them a revelation of God's grace and of the Son of God who died for them while they were still sinners.

XI

THE PROBLEM WITH JUDGING OTHERS

In the first chapter of Romans Paul painted the picture of the unrighteous pagan world and at the same time stated the case that the same corrupt and unrighteous activities were happening throughout the history of those who were under the Old Covenant of law. They were doing all the same unrighteous things that those who lived apart from the law were doing. This showed that the purpose, or we could say the mission, of the law was never to make people righteous. It is for this reason that Paul made the statement immediately after he finished this discourse on unrighteousness that those who are judging the pagan world for their unrighteousness really have no excuse for doing so when we see that Israel, who had the law, were doing exactly the same thing.

Paul was speaking to those within the early church in Rome who used the Bible as a weapon to cast judgement upon others and thought about it as a divine tool that everyone had to submit to, and follow the rules written within it, in order to become righteous. Consequently, since they naturally considered themselves to be 'under the mentality of following the written code of rules in the Bible,' they naturally considered themselves part of the 'righteous ones' and they most likely thought of the law with a confidence that it was indeed what makes people righteous; hence, they could therefore judge people who are unrighteous through using the Bible's words.

Paul made the radical statement that they actually had no right to do such a thing. In fact, he highlighted that when they did so, they were putting themselves in a very compromising situation by making the point that whenever they passed judgement on others they were really only condemning themselves.[41] How did Paul come to this conclusion?

I believe this was the basis of Paul's perspective. If you are actively judging people and using the written words in the Bible as your justification to do so then you first need to voluntarily put yourself under the mentality of the law. The logic continues that if you are doing that then clearly you must also be a sinner and a slave to sin because the law, as a written code, only leads someone to increase in sin. The law's power was in its ability to expose those who willingly placed themselves under it as unrighteousness. It never empowers man to actually be righteous nor was it intended to be used as a tool to beat an unbeliever into guilt. The law works against the very ones who want to use it to produce a righteous life by it. It reveals the inability of the one who believes they only need to follow its written instructions to be righteous.

---

[41] You, therefore, have no excuse, you who pass judgment on someone else, for at whatever point you judge the other, you are condemning yourself, because you who pass judgment do the same things. **Romans 2:1**

God himself told us through the prophet Isaiah what happens to people when they refuse to accept the true reality of God's message. When they would not accept that the Scriptures were given to lead them to Christ, then God's word would lose all power and simply become to them a rule book that was powerless to help them in any way regarding right living. As Isaiah testifies:

> *"to whom he said,*
> *"This is the resting place, let the weary rest";*
> *and, "This is the place of repose"—*
> *but they would not listen.*
> *So then, the word of the LORD to them will become:*
> *Do and do, do and do,*
> *rule on rule, rule on rule;*
> *a little here, a little there—*
> *so that they will go and fall backward,*
> *be injured and snared and captured."* **Isaiah 28:11-13**

The truth is we need to see that God's message in the Scriptures is one that proclaims the place of rest that is found in Jesus, the One whom we find rest for our souls. We need to allow the Spirit to reveal this message that is written in the Law and the Prophets. Trying to understand the Law and the Prophets without this perspective turns the Scriptures into letters on paper which Paul declares only brings about condemnation, sin, and death.[42]

---

[42] He has made us competent as ministers of a new covenant—not of the letter but of the Spirit; for the letter kills, but the Spirit gives life. **2 Corinthians 3:6**

Paul didn't make this thought up. It is written right there in Scripture. If you don't let the word of the Lord be about your resting place in Christ then the word of the Lord will just be a written code of: *"Do and do, do and do, rule on rule, rule on rule; a little here, a little there"* and the result of that perspective is a *"backward fall in faith, injured, snared, and captured"* in condemnation and sin.

I concede that the above statement is dramatic, extreme even, and a religious mind twister; however, it's the truth. When Christians in the body of Christ volunteer themselves under the law (that is in their thinking, for the battle is ultimately in the mind and it is our minds that need to be renewed in order to truly live in the freedom of God's grace[43]) in order that they can use it to cast judgement upon others, they are actually only exposing themselves as people who do the very things that they are bringing charges against. Perhaps not so blatant but the root of the sin will be equally active.

The reason for this is because when we come under the law we are first choosing to submit to something that is powerless to impart righteousness.[44] It's a tragic guarantee that we will only become more unrighteous because the law is powerless to help us outwork anything. However, when we live in God's grace and we are under grace then we are divinely empowered by grace and the result is grace that comes out of our life, and not judgement. When anyone chooses to live under the mentality of law, judgement comes out of their life and condemnation comes in because when they look to the root of the sin

---

[43] Do not conform any longer to the pattern of this world, but be transformed by the renewing of your mind. Then you will be able to test and approve what God's will is—his good, pleasing and perfect will. **Romans 12.2**

[44] For what the law was powerless to do in that it was weakened by the sinful nature, God did by sending his own Son in the likeness of sinful man to be a sin offering. **Romans 8:3**

they find themselves doing the very things they are condemning others for.

Paul talks about this in more detail in the seventh chapter of Romans. He addresses there how the law itself is a good and holy thing but that does not mean that it is going to cause you to outwork the 'God life' by being under it. Rather, it is good and holy at pointing you to the fact you cannot live the 'God life' unless you let go of the written code, the mentality that thinks God only needs to write down what he wants and that is enough to actually produce the desired results, and instead embrace the Spirit of Christ in you. The law's ultimate purpose was to lead mankind on a journey of recognising they would never achieve righteousness by zealously trying to follow a written code and they needed something more powerful. That is what the law was leading mankind to: to *the more powerful one* who is capable of living the righteous life in you, for you, and with you.

The whole letter is written to help the church understand the reality that just as it is vitally important to understand righteousness is a gift that came through God's grace, it's equally important to understand that the law does not and cannot make anyone righteous. In fact, anyone who comes under it hoping that it will manifest righteousness in them will only witness unrighteousness manifest.

Paul was showing the church that the law itself was a good thing but only in its correct context of being a voice that led mankind to see the need of Christ in our lives. When we think it is a good thing for helping us live, then tragedy manifests. It will only empower us to sin but it will be powerless to help us live a righteous life.

With this in mind, it is important that we as the church do not voluntarily yoke ourselves under the mentality of law because it will only empower us to sin and at the same time be powerless to give us any ability to be righteous. So then what should we do? Well, the good news for our life as the church, the body of Christ, is that we have been freed from sin; sin shall not be our master because we are not under law but under grace. Sin itself is not the problem in the Christian life. It is following the wrong leader that creates the problem – *even if that wrong leader is God's law*.[45] The only leader that will ensure a completely active and righteous life is Christ in us, our hope of glory.

When we look at our lives now as God's people, how do we want to outlive this life: with judgement or with grace? Paul was outlining that, as the church, we are in trouble if we choose the law and judgement. We need to actively choose the Spirit and grace. Grace needs to be the filter through which we see people because we know that people are powerless and without exemption when they don't have the Spirit of Christ Jesus living their life for them. Our own lives testify to this truth for now that we are in Christ we see Christ living our united life with him and it is a pure work of God's grace.

Such thoughts are not so easy to openly discuss together as a community; yet, Paul was purposely provoking the church to think about such things. This was the challenge Paul presented to those who were wielding God's written words in the Bible around in order to cast judgement on others: Why were they passing judgement on others when they were also doing what is wrong? Did they think it was a noble thing to present themselves perfect in public, using the Bible to publicly condemn others for their actions, yet remain captive to sin in private, living the life of a hypocrite? Paul sought to bring the church

---

[45] But if you are led by the Spirit, you are not under law. **Galatians 5:18**

back to their true foundation: it's far better to simply live by God's grace.

When we as the church choose to live by God's grace then we won't judge other people and we also won't be sinning. We will have grace for those who are weak and we ourselves will be empowered into obedience and righteousness to God. It's a far better offer God makes to us who are in Christ that we can have grace for others in their weaknesses and at the same time be personally empowered into the active life of God. It's a beautiful thing.

Paul revealed to the church that when we judge the world because of their ungodliness we are in fact *not* acting like God because it is not by God casting judgement upon people that causes them to repent; rather, it is his goodness, kindness, and patience that cause people to repent.[46]

God knows that pointing out sins to a sinner won't produce repentance and a change of heart. In fact, God testifies that this doesn't work through highlighting this very situation in the account of the fall of Adam and Eve. When God pointed out to Adam that he had broken God's command, did Adam then go onto repent and have a change of heart? No, not at all; instead, he went on to justify himself by putting the blame on God and on Eve. He said it was God who gave him the woman and it was the woman who led him to eat the fruit. Adam just shifted the blame. What about Eve? Did Eve repent and have a change of heart? No, she simply blamed the devil. She too found a way to simply shift the blame.

---

[46] Or do you show contempt for the riches of his kindness, tolerance and patience, not realizing that God's kindness leads you toward repentance? **Romans 2:4**

The truth is that pointing out sins doesn't cause someone to repent. It is not the revelation of their sin that causes people to repent; but rather, it is seeing how kind and patient God has been with them that causes them to repent. Likewise having a change of heart doesn't come out of having your sins exposed to you; but rather, by being made a new creation in Christ and having your sins washed away. When we receive a brand new heart that is full of the love of God, we naturally desire to walk in the ways of God's grace and love.

The example of Adam and Eve helps us see this point all the more clearer. If exposing their sins and judging them didn't cause repentance, even when it was God doing the judging, how much more can we be sure that we shouldn't judge others for their sins? What have we seen through the life of Jesus? We have seen the kindness of God, that when we were still unrighteous, ungodly, and wicked he sent his Son to die for us.[47] It is when we see this love that repentance comes forth: judgement doesn't bring anyone to repentance. Judgement only causes people to justify themselves but the grace of Jesus Christ, the gift of righteousness, and the love of God that comes through the life of Christ produces the desired results of a transformed life! When people taste of this wonderful reality and this kindness to them, you won't need to tell them to repent; they will bring themselves into the throne room of God to meet with him and not only repent but thank him for his free gift of his grace and love.

Paul was helping the church see there were two ways to outlive their Christian life. They could spend their life casting judgement on others or they could spend their life letting Christ's grace

---

[47] Very rarely will anyone die for a righteous man, though for a good man someone might possibly dare to die. But God demonstrates his own love for us in this: While we were still sinners, Christ died for us. **Romans 5:7-8**

be poured out through their lives into people in their world simply by having grace for them. The latter is the way we all should live because we know that God uses that same perspective to pour out his abundant grace upon us. We have the opportunity to have our lives marked for all eternity as lives of grace.

Now of course God is going to have grace for all of us. For we are, in Christ, sons and daughters of the living God. Paul spoke to the church and used some human arguments to help bring the church to a revelation that it was pointless to judge other people's actions and motives as it would only result in their own sins being exposed, resulting in becoming a slave to sin themselves.

The more we as the church can abound in grace, the more we can be assured that our lives will be free from sin. We can't help but do what is right when we are in Christ and living by his grace. This is important to understand because even as Christians there are two possibilities on how to live. We can be in Christ, but, instead of living by grace, still choose to live under the mentality of the law and harden our hearts in order to maintain that the list of 'do's and don'ts' as a means unto right godly living, in which case we will be terrible sinners. Perhaps we could still achieve a religiously appealing outer appearance; however, on the inside, the result would be a powerless Christian walk accompanied by a constant question of why we are, secretly, so captive to sin and condemnation.

This is the root of why it is so important to let the gospel of God's grace be the reality for our lives and to be free from the mentality of law. The law in its correct context allows us to appreciate its task in leading us to Christ but we can also leave it in the past in order to fully embrace our new covenant reality and relate with God in the new way of the Spirit. As Paul says:

But now, by dying to what once bound us, we have been released from the law so that we serve in the new way of the Spirit, and not in the old way of the written code. **Romans 7:6**

When a Christian doesn't accept the true purpose of the law, then a more religiously suitable understanding about the Law of Moses will be created in their mind, as well as the never ending additions of newly created laws and principles. The wrong understanding of law produces spiritual slavery in the lives of believers but it is not only the 'legalistic holiness mentality' that causes slavery. It is also any 'principle based mentality' that puts '*a principl*e' above the grace of Christ Jesus for your life.

A principle based mentality causes a believer to again listen to rules, laws, and principles that they can write down and read. It produces the mindset that if they can only follow and do those things then they will see the righteous, empowered Christian life outworked – but of course it fails. The truth is that when preachers try to help people obtain the Christ-life by pointing them to laws, keys, principles, and rules, instead of Christ himself and the grace that came through him, they do the body of Christ a terrible disservice.

Everything we do in our Christian life needs to come out of a spirit of grace. Everything is meant to be done out of a position of freedom, not from a position of spiritual obligation. Things such as reading the Bible and praying are not spiritual obligations. God doesn't demand these things from us: they are never a requirement.

When we start making laws out of things that are meant to be Spirit led actions, we unintentionally bring ourselves once more under the mentality of law. When we make laws for living the Christian life, we start making judgements upon not only the world but also our fellow Christian brothers and sisters.

As a community in Christ, we can only uplift Christ and his greatness, his glory and the power of his finished work. We need to put our confidence in the Spirit in us and trust that he will give us revelation on how to live and act. He is our teacher. He is the teacher *in us:* Christ in us, the hope of glory! We can have confidence that he will open up the Scriptures to give us understanding and he is also committed to leading us in the ways of his love so that we can live and relate with God and others according to God's heart of love.

A preacher's role is to simply lift up the greatness of Jesus and the result should be that the church has even more confidence in who they are in Jesus and who he is in them. The Spirit of God is your teacher in you: that is, Christ in you, your hope of glory.[48] You can come to Jesus and ask him for anything you need, any insight and wisdom you need and he will freely give it to you. When we live in the grace of God and the reality of his finished work, then we receive the abundance of eternal life and we begin to know both our Father and Jesus more and more. Eternal life, as defined by Jesus, is about the *'knowing'* of God as he truly is. This is the very reason we so openly let Jesus live his life in us by the power of his grace – because we want to know God. The result of letting Christ live in us and allowing his

---

[48] As for you, the anointing you received from him remains in you, and you do not need anyone to teach you. But as his anointing teaches you about all things and as that anointing is real, not counterfeit—just as it has taught you, remain in him. **1 John 2:27**

grace to be the supreme power in our lives is that we get to know our divine Father more and more intimately.

Now this is eternal life: that they may know you, the only true God, and Jesus Christ, whom you have sent. **John 17:3**

Paul understood that the people in the church were all growing in their revelation of Christ and his finished work. His desire was to continue to be a servant to them by helping them live more in God's grace and removing the false belief that God's *law* equals God's righteousness: instead he wanted to help them see the reality that God's *Son* equals God's righteousness! For Jesus has become for us wisdom from God, that is our righteousness, our holiness, and our redemption.[49]

---

[49] It is because of him that you are in Christ Jesus, who has become for us wisdom from God— that is, our righteousness, holiness and redemption. **I Corinthians 1:30**

XII

Leaving the Old to Enter the New

All who sin apart from the law will also perish apart from the law, and all who sin under the law will be judged by the law. **Romans 2:12**

If you want salvation, you need a covenant with God. This was a thought Paul wanted the church to understand and to understand it correctly. He again highlights how in the times of the ancient Israelites they had a covenant – the only available covenant: the Old Covenant of law and it was the only covenant available. They were in covenant with God and, subsequently, everybody else at that time was not in a covenant relationship with God.

Paul was explaining that those who were not a part of a covenant with God perished apart from a covenant. They couldn't even try to be righteous to earn salvation because they first needed a covenant: they had in essence, no hope. He went on and explained that it was also true that those who sinned under the law were also judged under the law in which case they would be found guilty of breaking the agreements of the covenant. So either way, mankind had a seemingly unfixable problem. If you were apart from the law you had no covenant and no hope. If you were Jewish you were under the law but also unable to live up to its requirements and thus equally falling short of the glory of God, being judged by the agreement of the covenant and and also found to be a sinner.

Paul explained that it didn't matter if one boasted about the law and put themselves under the law, the question was: did they obey the whole law? That meant *all* the law! If they didn't then they were not righteous. We can say, with absolute confidence, that not one person who attempted to obey the law, as a written code, could obey the whole law; therefore, there is no one who was righteous in that day just as there isn't anyone righteous today who voluntarily puts themselves under the law. Rather, we need to simply put ourselves under Christ so that he can declare us righteous because we belong to him and live a united life with him.

Paul showed us that the Israelites had the law; however, even though they had it and they knew it, it was still of no value to them to produce righteousness. He was also showing that even though the Gentiles had no covenant with God they still had within them an inherit understanding that God exists and that he has a way in which all men have been designed to live, and yet all men resist that way in order to follow the self-seeking way. Paul wanted to show that it was not in fact God's written code that illuminated the mind of man to the way of life God desires; rather, it is written in the DNA of all men.

But there was still an obvious problem, for regardless if men knew of God's ways from a written code or from an inner consciousness, both parties were still unable to translate the 'knowing' into an active righteousness. This of course, is because an active righteousness can only be given through the grace of God which has been God's plan all along.

What Paul truly wanted to discuss and explain, with great joy and anticipation, wasn't regarding the law or unrighteousness at all. He wanted to talk about God's grace and the righteousness that comes by faith; however, the church first needed to understand and accept how someone could be unrighteous before they could understand how someone becomes righteous.

So, although Paul's goal was to explain how someone is made righteous, the church first needed to understand how someone was considered unrighteous. Paul showed two ways that produced an unrighteous life. One way is by being under the law of God and the other is by having no covenant with God. So then, now that we know how someone can be unrighteous, how does someone actually become righteous? This is the point Paul is leading the church to understand. Revealing that the way someone can actually be righteous is by firstly understanding they need a covenant with God and the second point is to understand that that covenant needs to be the New Covenant of God's grace. It needs to be the covenant of God's Son, the covenant of his blood, the covenant of his power, the covenant of the Spirit of life, and not the Old Covenant of the written code.[50] The good news is that this New Covenant was now available to the entire world; both Jew and Gentile. He explained how the Gentiles could now for the first time receive a covenant with God. Remember, they didn't have the Old

[50] For this reason Christ is the mediator of a new covenant, that those who are called may receive the promised eternal inheritance—now that he has died as a ransom to set them free from the sins committed under the first covenant. **Hebrews 9:15**

Covenant and then enter the New Covenant. They had no covenant and yet now they could, through Christ, receive for the first time a covenant with God.

This is exactly the same for the Gentile world today, which is the vast majority of the whole world. We, as Gentiles, were never in the Old Covenant with God. We were a people who had no covenant with God. It's extremely important to understand that we never became Jewish and then became Christian. The truth is that we had no covenant with God. That means that we entered directly into the New Covenant of grace. *We were never under the Old Covenant of law.*

The coming of Christ and the finished work he completed upon the cross ushered in a new possibility for all of mankind to enter into God's eternal covenant. This New Covenant is available to all, both Jew and Gentile. To enter this covenant; however, meant leaving behind the old and entering into the new. The Jewish people of the time, although they indeed had a covenant, were required to leave their Old Covenant with God behind just as the pagans were required to leave behind their old pagan practices, pagan covenants and religious ideas, and, whether Jew or Gentile, enter into the New Covenant of God's grace. The pagans had to leave behind their pagan ideas, covenants with false gods, and pagan rituals to enter into the New Covenant; likewise, the Jews had to leave behind their Old Covenant and enter into the promised New Covenant.[51]

---

[51] For if there had been nothing wrong with that first covenant, no place would have been sought for another. But God found fault with the people and said: "The time is coming, declares the Lord, when I will make a new covenant with the house of Israel and with the house of Judah. It will not be like the covenant I made with their forefathers when I took them by the hand to lead them out of Egypt, because they did not remain faithful to my covenant, and I turned away from them, declares the Lord. **Hebrews 8:7-9**

So we see how God did not show favouritism; rather, he requires all men, whether Jew of Gentile, to enter the New Covenant – apart from their former covenants. The Jews had to leave behind the Old Covenant laws and traditions, and together with the Gentile believers, embrace the New Covenant that had been promised to them all throughout the Old Testament.

It certainly is good news to know that now whether we had a Jewish history or a Gentile history we have been made a new creation. We are neither Jew nor Gentile; rather, we are a new creation in Christ. We now live together in the New Covenant of God's grace.

For all of you who were baptised into Christ have clothed yourselves with Christ. There is neither Jew nor Greek, slave nor free, male nor female, for you are all one in Christ Jesus. **Galatians 3:27-28**

We need to rest in this reality and enjoy the truth of all Christ has completed on our behalf. He established the New Covenant to bless all of mankind so that we could relate and live with God as he truly is: the God of all grace. We as the body of Christ flourish when we understand the true attributes of grace as well as understanding the true purpose of the law. When we confuse grace with law we will live a confused and often burdened faith-walk. It is grace that is the empowerment to the righteousness of God. We should not be giving the law credit for that. The law was never the empowerment to the righteousness of God. The history of those under the law recorded in the Old Testament testifies to that. When we live in the grace of God, our own journey testifies to the truth that when we live in God's grace we also see the empowerment of God's grace at work in our lives.

XIII

What Gives Us Power?

Paul started the journey with the Roman church first by highlighting within Scripture the reality of Jesus both as a man and as God. He then presented, ever so briefly, the wonderful reality of righteousness by faith only to abruptly digress into the history of the Gentile world and also the history of Israel. His intention for doing so was to show how regardless if a person had a history that was apart from the law of God or they had a history where they were under the law of God it made no difference; everyone was unrighteous.

Paul then highlighted to the church how as Christians we shouldn't be using the written words in the Bible to cast judgment upon the world because it will only highlight to everyone who hears us that we ourselves are active in sin. This is because in order to use the written code to judge others you first need to neglect its true purpose as a testimony of God's grace and come under the false understanding of it being a rule book of do's and don'ts. This will always result in a powerless life with the knock on effect of living enslaved to sin;

however, when you are under grace then you are empowered to live a life of obedience in Christ Jesus. Paul continued and came to the point where he addressed what was most likely the main reason he wrote his letter to the Roman church in the first place.

Regarding this point, Paul was speaking specifically to the Jewish Christians in the church there who still held strongly to the law which justified their theology and judgemental actions on the law. In fact, it seems that they were attributing the benefits of *'Christ in us'* to *'the law'* which Paul sets out to expose as a terribly foolish thing to do.

Now you, if you call yourself a Jew; if you rely on the law and brag about your relationship to God; if you know his will and approve of what is superior because you are instructed by the law; if you are convinced that you are a guide for the blind, a light for those who are in the dark, an instructor of the foolish, a teacher of infants, because you have in the law the embodiment of knowledge and truth— you, then, who teach others, do you not teach yourself? You who preach against stealing, do you steal? You who say that people should not commit adultery, do you commit adultery? You who abhor idols, do you rob temples? You who brag about the law, do you dishonour God by breaking the law? As it is written: "God's name is blasphemed among the Gentiles because of you." **Romans 2:17-24**

Paul was speaking to Jewish Christians who were basically saying that they had an elite relationship with God because they had the Bible. In Paul's others letters, we often read how openly and passionately he opposes this perspective and here is no exception. Paul proclaims that our boast is not at all found in *the law* but rather in *the*

Lord; that is Jesus Christ the Lord. Jesus is the one we boast in and proclaim: the glorious riches of Christ. Our goal is to lift him up so that people may see him. Paul's perspective was that we as followers of Christ should be actively lifting him high in our lives so that those who are in darkness may see him high and exalted. We can joyfully lift up the life of Jesus in our thoughts and in our minds; likewise, preachers can lift up Jesus in their preaching and in their hearts that their hearers might see Christ. When people see Christ, then he can draw them out of their darkness and into his glorious light.

Paul, speaking to the church in Rome, was asking why in light of knowing Christ were they still boasting in the law? He was trying to highlight the foolishness of boasting in the law because he knew the law had no power to help do what is right. Attempting to use it to do what is right will only result in a fall into sin.

So Paul asked some basic questions. Did they really believe they were a guide for the blind because they had the instructions written down in the Bible? Did they really believe they were a light for those in the dark because they had the law? Did they really believe they were qualified to teach infants because they had the law as if the law is what made one mature in God? Did they really believe they were instructors of the foolish because they had, written in the Bible, the embodiment of knowledge and wisdom? In Paul's day and age, just as in our day and age, some members of the church were still putting their hope in the words found in the Bible for these realities instead of seeing that the reality of them were all were found in Christ.

My purpose is that they may be encouraged in heart and united in love, so that they may have the full riches of complete understanding,

in order that they may know the mystery of God, namely, Christ, in whom are hidden all the treasures of wisdom and knowledge.
Colossians 2:2-3

Paul testified throughout his life, over and over again, that 'in Christ' is the embodiment of knowledge and truth; not in 'the law'. In Jesus is the fullness of God's wisdom; not in the words written in the Bible. In Christ Jesus is where we see the expression of the full life of God; not in the law. The law was a testimony to the coming of Jesus but Jesus is the reality now at work in our lives. Christ is the teacher, the Spirit of Christ, who speaks to us and encourages that we can call God "Abba, Father!"

Paul was always putting his boast in Jesus and the grace that came through Jesus. In his letter to the Romans we find him speaking with people in the church who were putting their boast and hope in the Bible. It wasn't that they were not boasting in Jesus. It was just that they had two boasts – Jesus and the law. To Paul that was not only one too many boasts, it was actually a very destructive theology to hold.

Again, we need to remember to only give the law the attributes it deserves. It is absolutely true that it was good and holy; however, for what reason? It was good and holy because it led mankind to Jesus but it wasn't good and holy because it gave us the ability to be righteous by following it as a written code. *It never gave anyone the ability to be righteous and it never will*. It can still lead people to Jesus; however, not by them putting themselves under it; but rather, by them reading the testimony of the coming Christ and the promise of a New Covenant proclaimed within it which has now come to pass and is available to all. The Old Covenant law was only ever given to Israel; however, the promise of a coming Saviour that would save both Jew and Gentile, pay for all unrighteousness, and establish a New Covenant of the Spirit is testified to within the Scriptures for the benefit of all mankind.

Clearly, some of the early church in Rome did not understand the law in its true purpose. They failed to grasp its purpose as a divinely ordained guide to Jesus; rather, they were looking at it as God's rulebook that, when obeyed, produced righteousness.

Paul was highlighting that those in the church who were preaching rules, principles and laws, feeling it was their calling to tell other Christians what they should do, and the steps they needed to take to outwork their Christian lives were only exposing that they were breaking the very laws and principles they were teaching. Paul wasn't judging them; however, he was simply asking them to be honest and acknowledge if they were actually following the laws, rules, and moral ideas that they were preaching.

When preachers choose to preach principles, laws, and ideas, they will inevitably fail to do those very things themselves. Unless preaching is based on the reality of Christ, the fullness of his grace, and the power of his life, preaching is of no power. The power in preaching comes through the message of Jesus and the fullness of his grace. It is the truth that we are now holy, righteous, and blameless in him through his grace which empowers us to outlive the full life and will of God in a life that doesn't judge others or question people's motives; but rather, a life that is free to express the glorious love of God.

To truly live in the wide open spaces of God's love, we need a clear and correct understanding of the law. We are not against the law; *rather, we simply understand its true purpose*. This means we accept the law in its correct understanding: that it was a testimony that led mankind to Christ. We don't love the law thinking it's going to make us righteous. We love Jesus and we love the grace of Jesus Christ because he is the one who has made us righteous. He is not *making* us righteous. He has *already made* us righteous. We are righteous right now and right now he is the One who is outworking his very own life of righteousness in and through us.

Paul was challenging those in the church who were boasting in the law to really think about what they were doing because through preaching the law as the means of righteousness, they were really only exposing to the rest of the church that they were themselves sinners. It is a dramatic theory Paul puts forth but it is a profoundly real point he makes. *If you put yourself under the law, preach the law, and judge others by the words found in the Bible, you are only exposing that you are a sinner who is doing the very things you are judging others for.*

That's why it's better for us as Christians not to judge anyone, because we really don't want to do the things that we inherently know are not good things to be involved in. We can see the actions and weaknesses in people's lives and understand that they are not things we want to be enslaved by. We don't judge them for the very reason that we don't want to be enslaved by these things ourselves. It's better for us to have grace for them in their weakness and let *Christ in us* shine, allowing his kindness to lead them to repentance. This is a far more glorious perspective and outcome than pointing the finger and judging them. In this way people receive grace and they don't feel judged; rather, they feel the kindness of God being poured out through us and they themselves can come to God voluntarily, in repentance, and let the Spirit of God fill them with life. At the same time, we also are continually empowered unto life while sin loses its sting and has no power in our lives because we are not under law, but under grace.

XIV

THE DEEPER WORK OF GRACE

Circumcision has value if you observe the law, but if you break the law,
you have become as though you had not been circumcised.
Romans 2:25

As we read the letter to the Romans, we find Paul shift his focus onto some of the laws found in the Old Covenant: in particular, circumcision. It seems that there was still a strongly held viewpoint within the church that those who had been physically circumcised were, through that act, in right standing before God. We can make the assumption that some found Paul's teaching an offence as they felt he was minimizing the work God had done before the coming of Christ. Paul as usual, went out of his way to first establish that the law is indeed a good and holy thing when it's understood in the correct way. He never wanted to set the law up as if it was an enemy to the way of the Spirit. In saying this, it is important to once again stress the importance of understanding the law in its correct purpose as there are two ways the law can be interpreted and understood. One is God's divine way and the other is man's own established way. When the law is understood in its correct light it is indeed a friend to the gospel as it was a forerunner to Christ, proclaiming his coming and preparing the people to accept him. However, the wrong interpretation of the law that man established, will indeed lead people to stumble in their faith walk and this is a terrible tragedy. Paul goes into more details about these two separate views in Romans 9:

What then shall we say? That the Gentiles, who did not pursue righteousness, have obtained it, a righteousness that is by faith; but Israel, who pursued a law of righteousness, has not attained it. Why not? Because they pursued it not by faith but as if it were by works. They stumbled over the "stumbling stone." **Romans 9:30-32**

The truth is that whenever anyone looks to the Bible as a rulebook or a life manual with the expectation of following its rules and principles to outwork a godly life, they will find themselves stumbling over the grace of God. People who hold onto the wrong idea of the law end up furious with those who uphold the grace of God because it is grace that keeps tripping them up! They want to earn a right standing from God and they want others to earn it too! However, the truth is that righteousness by faith is God's divine way and it is glorious when you can accept it but terribly offensive when you want to maintain the false understanding of the law.

Paul, using the example of circumcision, went on to explain that it wasn't in following rituals that positioned someone in right standing with God; rather, it was by living by the Spirit of love that positions someone in right standing before God. Christ is the love of God, for he is God himself. It is his loving ways that are being outworked within us that God sees and that God approves of.

Clearly, legally binding obligations from the written code don't position anyone in the right light before God. They were all only a shadow to help us understand the greater reality of Christ. In their time God honoured their purpose as a shadow of the reality to come; however, now that the reality has come, God's desires are outworked by the Spirit of his love in us. God has made the way possible where all of us can fulfil the way of his love because he has placed the Holy Spirit in us. He has placed the Spirit of love within us to empower us and to actually live with us and for us! The good news continues to flourish in our lives as we see that it is Jesus himself who positions us in the right light before God. It is Jesus who empowers us to outwork God's love, grace and truth in this world. It is in Jesus that we find our identity as God's children.

Paul was making the point that God looked with favour upon those who outworked the nature of love in their lives and not those who simply followed external rules. An internal reality of love is what God has always desired; not an external façade. Who can outwork the nature of God except those who allow that very nature to operate in their lives by grace? For it was by works once again that all men would fail; however, when we allow it to be by grace, all men can see the nature of God in them flourish. We are to simply allow Christ in us to be our very real reality and let the grace of God pour out of us. Those who live a life of love are the people that God looks upon with favour and when we let God's grace have control that is exactly the kind of life we find ourselves living. Some members of the Roman church had difficulty with such a simple, yet logical position. The law as a rulebook and the means to a right standing before God was so ingrained into their thinking that it seemed a great hurdle to overcome.

Paul wanted the church to see this deeper truth: God is doing a work *within* his people. Through the coming of Christ and the New Covenant, he established a universal shift in man's possibilities that had taken place. Now man actually had the Spirit of God *at work within him.* The focus was not to be on how much man could do for God but on how much God, now in man, could do! Christ now lives in us and this reality means that we truly have a hope of glory.

Paul was unpacking this reality. God had now given something so much bigger and more glorious than a written code to the early church. The Spirit of the living God was now at work in the believer and when the believer allowed this act of grace to take place, God's nature in the believer could truly shine. The New Covenant of the Spirit has the ability to do in the life of a believer all the things the Old Covenant of a written code never could.

He was helping the church to understand that we now live our life out of a revelation of Christ. This is an inner reality that transforms the external not through following a rulebook; but rather, by allowing the Holy Spirit to outlive his life of grace within us. We don't look at other believers for what they have done in their outer position to be right before God; but rather, we look at what God has done in them. Jesus has baptised them into his death, Jesus has raised them in his resurrection into his life, and now they are no longer the old self but they have been made a new creation. The old is gone, the new has come, and all of this is to the glory of God. This perspective doesn't receive praise from man because man still only sees the earthen vessel from the outside; however, it does receive praise from God because God sees the new creation on the inside. To God, that is a beautiful thing.

XV

THE HISTORY OF GOD AND MAN

The letter to the Romans not only aimed at helping the church understand the concept of a righteousness by faith but also to help them understanding the history of God in light of the reality of Christ. For many in the church, especially those who came from a Jewish background, there was a need to clarify how Jesus and the New Covenant of grace fit into the whole narrative of the Scriptures. The following is what I believe to be Paul's perspective on Scriptural history in the light of the Christ reality.

God originally set the nation of Israel apart and made an exclusive covenant with them for the very purpose that, through first establishing an exclusive covenant, a way could be made to introduce an inclusive covenant – that is, a covenant available to all mankind. The initial covenant, that was exclusive, had always been planned to be temporary. Its primary purpose was to create the opportunity for God to proclaim that the coming of his eternal inclusive covenant, when it arrived in its appointed time, would be made available to every nation. The Old Covenant was made with just one nation but through it was testified the coming New Covenant that would be available for every nation. This is the good news of Jesus Christ: that his grace is sufficient for the whole world, whether Jew or Gentile, and we all are welcome to be included in this covenant.

The Gentiles were given the freedom to create their own 'covenants and gods' while Israel was obligated to religiously fulfil the traditions and rituals of the Old Covenant that God had made with them. It was through this that both Jew and Gentile found themselves attached to covenants based on works and it was through the coming of Christ that all mankind, whether Jew or Gentile, were required to leave their 'covenants of works' and enter into God's covenant of grace.

Before the full plan of God had been revealed, it was easy for the Gentile nations to claim God was being unfair towards them because the one true God had seemingly left them with no covenant and no hope. Then, after the coming of Christ, the Jews may have felt that it was unfair that they were now expected to let go of the old, temporary covenant in order to enter into the new, eternal covenant. It showed that God truly did not show favouritism. So whether you were a Jew or Gentile, there was the letting go of the old before the entering into the new. A great challenge for both Jew and Gentile in doing this was that all their traditions and rituals that had set them apart and given them their identity would have to be left behind. There was much that they would have been happy to leave behind, but there were also a lot of things I'm sure they liked. There were some parts of their Old Covenant that they didn't think of as being legalistic; but rather, as enjoyable religious rituals. These things too could not be transferred into the New Covenant as the New Covenant was not one that could be recognised by the rituals and ceremonies; but rather, by the outworking of the new nature within them. The rituals and ceremonies that had to be left behind were only shadows pointing to Christ; however, now they, together with every other nation, could freely received the reality God had always intended all of mankind to have.

Paul spent a lot of time explaining the history of God in order for his hearers to understand what God was doing in their time in history. It had already been explained to the church that throughout the course of history both Jew and Gentile had clearly been unrighteous. This was something that I am sure came as a complete shock to many in the church as it was not a standard historical theology but radically different. Yet, Paul gives such a clear and irrefutable defence to his thoughts and theology and does it all with such a spirit of love that I image he indeed brought his hearers to agree to his understanding of not only the gospel but God's divine plan seen in the Scriptures.

Paul showed his fellow Jewish believing brothers that when they looked at their history they could see that their forefathers were exactly the same and at times even worse then those who did not have the law so how could they therefore think the law was the answer for the unrighteous to become righteous? He was helping the Jewish believers in the church see how the law never helped their own people be righteous. His intention was to reveal that if it failed to produce righteousness for those whom it was given to, how much more would if fail to produce righteousness in the lives of outsiders of the Old Covenant? Indeed, how much more would it fail to bring righteousness to those now in the New Covenant? The law will never be a successful tool used to force people into righteousness; rather, it will only succeed in pushing people into more unrighteousness. Paul found it of the highest importance to outline the how both Jew and Gentile had a history of being unrighteous. One had a covenant of law and the other had no covenant; however, both had the same unrighteous result.

Paul already knew the question that would be asked in responds to these new revelations from his Jewish brothers. That question was: *'what advantage is there in being a Jew then?'* I believe it is a legitimate and genuine question that the Jewish believers of the day most likely asked. If, after all, their exclusive Old Covenant of law was brought to an end and they were now in a covenant where they were on the exact same level as the Gentiles, was there any benefit whatsoever in being Jewish in the first place? After all they had gone through in their Jewish history, the very things they endured and were now so proud of, did God now want them to let that go? I'm sure that it clearly made sense to them that God wanted the pagans to let go of their pagan religious rituals and traditions, but they were pagan rituals and the Jewish people had God's rituals! These were rituals and traditions that God had given them. Did they really have to equally, just like the Gentiles, leave them all behind and enter the promised New Covenant? If this was the case, was there any benefit in even being born a Jew? Paul seemed to think so. Not regarding any right standing before God; but rather, to enjoy the fact that God choose their nation to be the forerunner through which salvation could be granted to the whole world.

Paul was helping the church understand that although it's true that the Old Covenant with its traditions and rituals was given by God, it was also necessary for the church to understand its purpose in light of the revelation of Jesus. The truth is that all the rituals, laws, and ceremonies were created to be examples of the spiritual reality we now have in Christ: the truth was that everything in the Scriptures has always been about Jesus. From God's divine perspective nothing finds its value and purpose outside of Christ: everything finds its value in him.[52]

It is now that we, whether Jew or Gentile, have been brought into Christ that we can see these laws, rituals, and traditions found in the Scriptures as shadows[53] and types of Christ.[54] They have enormous value when we see them in this light; however, in and of themselves, apart from understanding the 'Christ story' in them, they are temporal obligations that have already passed away. The value they still hold for us today is the hidden story of Jesus within them now revealed as now the veil has been removed and we can see the light of Christ within the Scriptures. Now that we have entered into Jesus we can look back at them and see the Christ story within them. They are great at testifying to the present reality of Christ; however, they are no longer an on-going ritual, tradition, or requirement that we are obligated to do. Whenever we read the Old Covenant, it's important to always understand our New Covenant reality within it. It is never to be thought of as a rule book; rather, it is the testimony of Christ, his suffering on our behalf, and his glories we now partake in through the working of his grace.

---

[52] His intent was that now, through the church, the manifold wisdom of God should be made known to the rulers and authorities in the heavenly realms, according to his eternal purpose which he accomplished in Christ Jesus our Lord. In him and through faith in him we may approach God with freedom and confidence. **Ephesians 3:10-12**

[53] The law is only a shadow of the good things that are coming—not the realities themselves. **Hebrews 10:1**

[54] Therefore do not let anyone judge you by what you eat or drink, or with regard to a religious festival, a New Moon celebration or a Sabbath day. These are a shadow of the things that were to come; the reality, however, is found in Christ. **Colossians 2:16-17**

XVI

WHAT ABOUT BEING JEWISH THEN?

So what advantage is there in being Jewish? Paul gives quite an enthusiastic response declaring that there was 'much in every way!' But why, you ask? Paul clarifies by stating that, for starters, out of the entire world, they were the first people to be entrusted with the very words of God. This was a divine blessing that the Jewish nation received. The Jewish nation themselves were no better than the Egyptians or any other nation group of the time. They weren't chosen because of their works as righteous people: they were chosen by grace.

Although they were given a covenant that, in essence, they were destined to fall short of God's glory in, it was still an incredible blessing that God did not let them run off like every other nation; rather, God prophesied the coming of Jesus through the their covenant Scriptures. Paul talked about the covenant of law as, for those within it, a prison that kept them united in a relationship with the one true God until faith would come. We see throughout the Scriptures how they were doing all sorts of terrible, ungodly things but they still did not escape from a covenant relationship with God. God was keeping them imprisoned, so to speak, in a relationship with him, even though it was not working because God's desire was to keep them with him until the point where he could give them their promised Saviour who the entire Law and the Prophets constantly prophesied about.[55] God knew when they accepted Christ they would finally enter into a covenant that would work gloriously. A covenant that was not based on man's desire for a work's relationship; but rather, a covenant based on the very nature of God: *a grace based relationship.* God kept them in a relationship with him so that they could, in the end, enter into their true inheritance: that is the New Covenant life. A faith walk in their promised New Covenant where they would have the revelation of God's perfect love for them, that God would not withhold his only begotten Son from them but give him up freely in order that they could finally see their God in his true light: the God of all grace.

Paul was explaining that the Jewish people were greatly blessed because they were given the very words of God. The Jewish people were led to expect, and ultimately accept, the coming Christ by the prophetic Scriptures given to them in the Old Covenant. It was through the testimony of the Scriptures that the promised New Covenant opened up, for the first time, a way for Gentiles as well as Jews to become God's covenant people. Gentiles never had to go into the Old Covenant of law to be led to Christ because they benefited from the journey the Jewish nation took, in essence, to bless the whole world. The Jewish nation was given the honour of taking the journey

---

[55] Before this faith came, we were held prisoners by the law, locked up until faith should be revealed. So the law was put in charge to lead us to Christ that we might be justified by faith. Now that faith has come, we are no longer under the supervision of the law.
Galatians 3:23-25

with God first and, through that journey, allowed God the opportunity to introduce Jesus to the whole world. The good news is that Gentiles can enter directly into God's Eternal Covenant of grace.

The reason the Gentile world was and is so greatly blessed is because God first called the Jewish nation and gave them the law through which he could prophesy about the promise of a Messiah, not only for the Jewish nation but also a light for the Gentiles, and through the Scriptures make known the coming of the Christ who would establish the New Covenant. The Old Covenant gave God the opportunity to prophesy about the good news that would be given, and the righteousness by faith that would be for all from first to last. God used the relationship with the Jewish nation that he had with them, through the covenant of law, to give a testimony that the whole world could look to and realise God's ultimate intention. It allowed God to give to mankind their Saviour and also show mankind how he had been promised for thousands of years. It is because of the journey God first took with the Jewish nation that the whole world inherently knows that the true God has been testifying about himself and his plans concerning mankind throughout the Scriptures. The Scriptures testify about the coming Messiah to the whole world.

The law can lead a Gentile to Christ because the Holy Scriptures testify openly about the coming of a Saviour that will be for all of mankind and that he would come to save all mankind through first being prophesied through the Jewish nation. The Scriptures also testify that when the Christ comes and God establishes his New Covenant the Jewish nation would also be expected to enter the New Covenant and be equals with everyone else who enters this New Covenant. In the Old Covenant, Israel was the whole part. They had an exclusive covenant with God. However, even in that covenant God spoke of the New Covenant to come that would include both Jew and Gentile. In the New Covenant, Israel would be an equal part along with the Gentiles, such as is illustrated by them becoming a third, together with Egypt and Assyria, who represent the ungodly Gentile world that Paul presented in the first chapter of Romans:

In that day Israel will be the third, along with Egypt and Assyria, a blessing on the earth. The LORD Almighty will bless them, saying, "Blessed be Egypt my people, Assyria my handiwork, and Israel my inheritance." **Isaiah 1924-25**

"It is too small a thing for you to be my servant to restore the tribes of Jacob and bring back those of Israel I have kept. I will also make you a light for the Gentiles, that you may bring my salvation to the ends of the earth." **Isaiah 49:6**

What Paul was sharing was that, although now in the light of Christ there is no different between Jew and Gentile, the Jewish people could still consider it an enormous blessing to be the nation through which this salvation came to the whole world. Even Jesus, when he walked the earth, testified that salvation comes through the Jews.[56] Their nation was God's chosen vessel for the whole world to be blessed by first choosing the Jewish nation as an act of his grace to be his covenant people. Even though it proved to be a pattern of disobedience because they were trying to relate to God based on

---

[56] You Samaritans worship what you do not know; we worship what we do know, for salvation is from the Jews. **John 4:22**

works, which always leads to disobedience, they are still blessed because God had chosen them. Although they were disobedient, God didn't judge them for this because in his foreknowledge he knew they would fail just as he knew the Gentiles, without a covenant with him, would fail. He withheld his judgement for both those who were under the covenant of law and those who were apart from a covenant until the coming of Christ. Then he put the judgement upon Christ for all the unrighteousness that took place by both the Jew and the Gentile.

God presented him as a sacrifice of atonement, through faith in his blood. He did this to demonstrate his justice, because in his forbearance he had left the sins committed beforehand unpunished — he did it to demonstrate his justice at the present time, so as to be just and the one who justifies those who have faith in Jesus.
Romans 3:25-26

Now that Christ has been given and he is available to both Jew and Gentile, all can freely come to Christ and receive the New Covenant. Those who are Jewish need to leave behind the Old Covenant where they lived by the law and Gentiles need to leave behind their own laws, religions, and idols. Now with everything left behind, together we can all come into Christ receiving God's eternal, glorious covenant where the Spirit of God comes to make his home in us where we can find our mutual identity not in our past religions but in our present covenant of Grace. Our identity is no longer found in different religions, rituals or covenants – it is now found *in Christ*.

XVII

Explaining Grace in Context

It seems correct to assume that Paul often had people ask him questions after they heard him preach the good news of the righteousness that comes by faith. I'm sure it would have been a normal expectation for him that people would question his message; therefore, it is not surprising to find at this point of the letter Paul re-quoting some previously asked questions in order to help his current audience who most likely had similar questions racing through their minds.

This too, is an important perspective for those who are preachers to understand. The preacher's role is to proclaim the good news of Jesus Christ, the greatness of who he is, the power of his finished work upon the cross, the empowerment of his grace, and the new way of the Spirit. As a preacher does this, it's okay, and should even be expected, that the listener will then have questions and may even initially misunderstand what is being communicated. Preachers should always have confidence to re-explain the gospel in context to the questions people ask. We can explain the 'Jesus story' throughout all the Scriptures and it is also possible to present it again in context to the questions that are raised.

Sometimes people see Paul giving practical instructions in his letters and interpret that to mean that preachers should be following this pattern of giving practical advice; however, what we need to recognise is that Paul's practical instructions always came out of first simply preaching the reality of the gospel. It was after the gospel was proclaimed that the early church then asked questions about how the gospel message worked within a specific part of their lives. Paul then helps them understand their particular situation in the light of the reality of Jesus and the gospel of God's grace. There is nothing wrong with doing this but it's important to know that we can't preach practical advice just for the sake of it. Rather we need to be preaching the good news to the saints and as they have questions that come out of hearing the gospel, we then can share the gospel once more in context to their question.

It is also vitally important to understand how essential the gospel is for believers to hear. The gospel is not a message for the lost. It is a message for the church. That may sound strange to you because it is not often said, but, I assure you, it's the truth. Just look at Paul as the prime example. He was constantly preaching and explaining, then re-explaining, the gospel to the churches throughout his letters. Of course Paul also shared the gospel with unbelievers, as illustrated throughout Acts, but Paul preached the good news to the lost in order that they could also live in the reality of the gospel of God's grace. Paul, however, spent the majority of his time preaching the gospel to the church. He did this because the gospel message is one that is for the believer and it is something that those in Christ need to continually hear and have a forum where they can also ask related questions in order to grow in their confidence in it. Paul was always preaching the good news of God's grace to those who had already accepted it because he knew that it was a message that the church needed to always find their foundation in and only through staying grounded in its truth could they truly reap the benefits of a life empowered by God's grace.

There is at the core of the gospel message an invitation to the lost to come into this good news of God's grace; however, it is important to remember that the gospel is still the believer's reality. *Grace is not just a message. It is a place in which we live.* When we become part of the body of Christ we enter into our new home: the beautiful kingdom of God's grace. It is important that we always keep this point fresh in our minds. The gospel of God's grace is a message that is needed for the church to hear as it is those who already believe that need to continually be refreshed by hearing the good news. Granted, it is an invitation that is given and made available to the whole world; however, those who are called to preach need to be aware they are preaching God's message to the believer in Jesus in order to establish them in the reality of God's grace and help them to grow in it, truly grasp it, and remain in it. It is also important that preachers are open to answer questions from believers that arise from preaching the radical reality of God's good news.

Those who opposed Paul's gospel had, so it seems, a common fault in their stand. They often looked at what Paul was saying, not as a living reality, but as a theory that could be broken down and thus disproven. They made it all systematic in their minds without allowing the reality of the message he was presenting resonate in their hearts. Paul explained in his letter to the Romans that in order to help the church understand the divine reality of God's message, he sometimes had to revert to using human arguments to answer questions that were themselves based on human thinking. Those who often challenged his message were making their charge based on human, systematic thinking. Paul, on the other hand, always endeavoured to bring his listeners back to the point that the gospel is real. It's not just a theology. It is a profound reality.

We should allow the truth of the gospel message to not just be theological points we agree with but a living, wonderful, reality in our hearts and minds. Jesus, the son of the living God, really did die for us, we really were baptised with him in his death, we really died with him, he really was raised for our justification, and we really were raised with him; thus, the Spirit of the living God has really been placed in us to be the empowerment of our lives. When we accept that all these points are not merely theories but profound realities we truly start to understand the heart of God and rest in our mutual inheritance in Christ.

The gospel is not a theory: it is a glorious reality. If the same Spirit that created the universe and raised Christ Jesus from the dead, if that very same Spirit now lives in you, then I can say with absolute confidence, as a sibling in Christ, that you are a spiritual person who walks in the way of the Spirit. The Spirit of God in you will empower you into all obedience, into all God's will, and into a fruitful, God glorifying life. Why am I confident that this is a certainty? Because the gospel is real and it's really true what happened to you at the point of salvation. You really have been made a new creation and you can rest in that truth with full confidence.

Paul expressed in his letter to the Romans how some other believers are slandering him and his preaching. How they were not hearing what he said as a reality but instead talking it as only a theory and missing the whole point of his message.

Why not say — as we are being slanderously reported as saying and as some claim that we say — "Let us do evil that good may result"? Their condemnation is deserved. **Romans 3:8**

People were coming to Paul, challenging the gospel he preached and the message he was declaring; the message that we are, in Christ, righteous by faith and not by works. Paul declared that God now looks at us and calls us righteous because we are now living in his Son who is the righteousness of God. Some people heard Paul's message but instead of accepting it within the framework of it being a divine reality, they rejected it as a living reality and instead dissected it as a lifeless theory; thus, looking for holes in his message in order to come back and ask questions, not to grow in their understanding of grace but to minimize and dismiss the actual work of Jesus. They sought to bring it all down to a theological babble level: a theological discussion that was only based on possible theories.

The foundational accusation against Paul was that he was preaching that Christians could do whatever they wanted, as much as evil as they liked, and God would still make good things happen anyway. Paul said those kinds of accusations against him were coming from preachers and church leaders who were taking their stand upon

123

the law because any preacher who has an inherent distrust of the message of grace always seeks his authority from the law. Because of this, Paul knew that they were feeling condemned for making such accusations because if they were putting themselves under the law then they were in a place of powerlessness to do what was right. They were trying to destabilise the church in their foundation of grace largely because they did not understand it themselves and they did not want to look foolish before the church so they hid behind the written code of God.

Paul, in response to these slanderous reports about him, actually makes a statement that he knows his accusers must feel self-condemned for doing so. It wasn't that God was condemning them; rather, it was the condemnation they were creating in their own minds due to yoking themselves under the law. Paul said this because these particular preachers were minimizing the reality of the gospel and taking away the confidence of the Spirit. They were slandering the message that would bring liberty, obedience, and righteousness to the body of Christ so they could both justify themselves and defend both their theological and self-appointed authoritarian positions.

Paul wasn't interested in his reputation.[57] He was interested in preaching the gospel and making a stand for its truth. He was seeking to establish the body of Christ in its glorious reality. One of the greatest challenges he faced was his main point in the letter to the Romans: bringing members of the church out of the religious assumption that the law was God's tool to make man righteous; meaning that they believed the law was the hope of the world

---

[57] Am I now trying to win the approval of men, or of God? Or am I trying to please men? If I were still trying to please men, I would not be a servant of Christ. **Galatians 1:10**

regarding a transformation into righteousness. Paul spent his life helping the church get established in the truth that it was in fact 'Christ in us' who is the hope of the world: the hope of glory.

A message about morals and a righteousness that was obtained through following a written code of works was not offensive to anyone; however, a message about morals and righteousness that came as a *gift of grace apart from diligently following a written code* was fervently opposed. Paul pressed on in spite of the persecution from other Christian leaders and preachers because he understood that the only thing that will actively stop the empowering work of God's grace in a believer's life is their stubborn refusal to let go of the wrong understanding of the law.

Let us today take the teaching Paul shared throughout the letter to the Romans to heart. We all at some point in our faith-walk need to come out of the religious mindset that believes the coming under and following of the law will result in a righteous life and journey into the understanding that it is Christ, who lives in us, who is the Saviour unto us and that we can now walk in him as righteous.

The Gentiles without the law were unrighteous, and Israel, who had the law, were also unrighteous. Neither group obtained righteousness in their own efforts but where mankind failed and fell short of the glory of God, Jesus succeeded on mankind's behalf, giving righteousness to all who believe as a gift of his grace. The law was never given as a guide for righteous rules of living. It was given as a guide to the righteous one – to Jesus! The law is like a prophet not a principle. If we seek to understand it apart from its testimony of Jesus we will only find useless words that have no power to impart the strength needed to live a life of love.

We could look at this today within the church at some who hold strongly to the idea that the law found in the Old Covenant is a good and holy thing for the Christian to hold on to, to observe, and to keep as a good rule book for Christian living. If we find ourselves holding to this position we too need to let it go. Let go of the wrong idea of the law and embrace the truth. The law, when we try to live under it and preach it, will only make us sinful; hence, empowering us to sin while giving us no power to be righteous. What we need to do is come into this reality of a righteousness that is by faith. It is now that both Jew and Gentile can come into this glorious New Covenant of grace. A covenant for all that can do what the Old Covenant could not do: empower us unto righteousness.

It is clear that many in the early church didn't accept this way of thinking so easily and persisted in the need of the law. Paul, taking the opportunity to make his case even clearer that that was not so, quotes Scripture from the law to highlight why we should not believe the law is something for us to boast in.

> *"There is no one righteous, not even one;*
> *there is no one who understands;*
> *there is no one who seeks God.*
> *All have turned away,*
> *they have together become worthless;*
> *there is no one who does good, not even one."*
> *"Their throats are open graves;*
> *their tongues practice deceit."*
> *"The poison of vipers is on their lips."*
> *"Their mouths are full of cursing and bitterness."*

"Their feet are swift to shed blood;
ruin and misery mark their ways,
and the way of peace they do not know."
"There is no fear of God before their eyes."

Now we know that whatever the law says, it says to those who are
under the law, so that every mouth may be silenced and the whole
world held accountable to God. Therefore no one will be declared
righteous in God's sight by the works of the law; rather, through the
law we become conscious of our sin. **Romans 3:10-20**

We need to pay particular attention to what Paul says immediately following this collection of Old Testament quotes. He explained that everything written in the law was not written for those outside of its covenant but for those within it. This particular Scripture, therefore, was not written regarding the Gentile world but to those who were under the law. When we read this Scripture again with this understanding fresh in our minds we can see it in a totally different light, for, according to Paul, its correct meaning states:

"There is no one righteous, not even one who is under the law;
there is no one under the law who understands;
there is no one under the law who seeks God.
Under the law, all have turned away,
they have together, under the law, become worthless;
there is no one, under the law, who does good, not even one."
Under the law their throats are open graves;

under the law their tongues practice deceit."
Under the law, the poison of vipers is on their lips.
Their mouths, under the law, are full of cursing and bitterness.
Under the law their feet are swift to shed blood;
under the law, ruin and misery mark their ways,
and under the law, the way of peace they do not know.
Under the law there is no fear of God before their eyes."

This is a very bold statement but as we read it over again and be honest with what Paul is saying we have to come to this conclusion. Paul was explaining that when you have God's holy law, or when a Gentile has their own idea of a holy law, the only thing it does is cause accusation and judgement upon other people while at the same time cause a complete misunderstanding regarding God's true nature and character.

The greatest acts of evil have historically been perpetrated based on some form of holy law and most of those came from taking the law found in the Bible: God's actual written law. This of course was never the reason for the law being given. It does, however, highlight to us why God doesn't want Christians to be able to use his words written in the Bible to judge others and justify their own condemning agendas in the new era of grace. The Bible when used to judge others' motives and actions is so easily mistreated. Although good and holy, when used as a written code, it can easily be used to justify wicked and cruel acts.

The reality is the law will only silence those who try to use it to judge others because it will only highlight that they are also sinning since the law was not written to those who live apart from it but for those who place themselves under it. If you want to use the words written in the Bible to condemn, you are placing yourself under false understanding of those very words and bringing about your own self-condemnation in the process. Isn't it incredible what Paul was saying? He was testifying that the law was never written to the Gentiles who did not have the law. It was actually written to those who were under the law. It was written to highlight the problem of looking to a written code to understand righteousness instead of looking to the Son of God to understand righteousness. Understanding this will help you to *not* put your trust in the law as a tool that can be used to make someone righteous.

It is because we are not under the law but under grace that we can live without sin. It is grace that has saved us from a sinful life. The law, on the other hand, when used as a written code, will pull a believer back into condemnation and from there into sin.

Under the law is not a good place to be. In our religious mind it sounds great but the reality is the law is powerless to help us do anything right. That role of positive transformation belongs to the Spirit in us. When we live in the grace of God, in the Spirit of God, and in the power of what Jesus did for us, then in that place of grace we are empowered to outlive a life that is in total obedience to God. Thank God we are not under the law but under grace and now can live, not as a theory but as a living reality, in God's obedience.

XVIII

LIVING BY THE SPIRIT

Therefore no one will be declared righteous in God's sight by the works of the law; rather, through the law we become conscious of our sin. **Romans 3:20**

Paul explained that no one will be declared righteous in God's eyes by following the law so why would we, as the church today, want to put the yoke of the law on our necks and the necks of unbelievers in our world? This problem of the law as a rule book can be seen throughout the Scriptures, which is where Paul is getting all of his thoughts from. Indeed, when we look back to when the law was first given we can see this same situation being played out through the Jewish people coming into a covenant of grace with God through Abraham; but then, rather than living by grace they wanted to live by works; and so, desiring a covenant based on their works, God gave it to them through Moses.

It is a tragic belief system to think the only thing one needs is the instructions from God and they can do the rest. Is that all we need?

Do we just need God to give us written instructions? *What has God truly given us?* He has given us the Spirit to abide in us! He has given us his Son to abide in. God has given us *what we truly need*. Not a written code but his Spirit. That is why now under grace we can not only *know* what is right but also have the *empowerment* within us to outlive it.[58] The Israelites, representing the collective misunderstanding of mankind's mindset, thought that God only needed to give them his instructions. They didn't understand that what they really needed was God's Spirit. Instructions from God, without the Spirit of God, will not help anyone to be righteous. The Spirit of God, without written instructions; however, is powerful enough to lead everyone into righteousness. The Spirit of God in us is more than enough to talk to us, to instruct us in his ways of love, and direct us in God's ways.

God gave the Israelites a written code that they could attempt to live by in order to be righteous. What transpired directly after this happened? They broke all the laws! They indulged in sexual immorality and other debauchery going so far as to even build a golden calf and calling it God!

Moses came down the mountain and through the law exposed their shame causing the whole community to become conscious of their sinfulness. The purpose of the law, therefore, was not given as a written instruction manual on how to be righteous but to help them realise that they were unrighteous. It was not given to help them be righteous but to silence their boasting in their own works so that they could be led to the one who they were meant to find their boast in:

---

[58] May the God of hope fill you with all joy and peace as you trust in him, so that you may overflow with hope by the power of the Holy Spirit. **Romans 15:13**

Jesus Christ, the righteousness of God who imparts, as a gift, righteousness to all who believe upon him.

But now apart from the law the righteousness of God has been made known, to which the Law and the Prophets testify. **Romans 3:21**

The above Scripture was an extremely important statement that Paul declared. In his letter, Paul had up to this point of the letter explained how the law does not make people righteous. The law does not help people to be righteous by following it. The law itself will only empower people to be unrighteous if they yoke themselves under it. He then goes on to say that now the righteousness that we all want has now been made known and this righteousness is from God, apart from the written instruction code of the law. Obtaining this righteousness has nothing to do with the law; and yet, the law, acting as a prophetic voice, testifies to this truth.

How amazing that the law itself testifies that we need to embrace Christ and not the law. The Prophets testify that we need to embrace Christ and not the Prophets. Embrace Christ for he is the very righteousness you desire. Embrace Jesus alone, apart from the law and the Prophets, who has been given to you. The law and the Prophets are actually imploring us to live that reality.

The law has never been an enemy to the gospel. Law and grace are not counterproductive. The false understanding of the law, however, as a rule book and a works righteousness idea to obtain a right standing with God, is against grace. That false understanding is directly opposed to grace and the two cannot live in the same realm. But the law in its proper form was given to testify to the coming of the

Christ and lead people to him. The law itself testifies that there is no righteousness in itself but it lifts up and proclaims the reality of the one all of mankind can now be connected to. The law could never impart righteousness but it continually proclaimed the coming of the one who could! The law's divine ministry has always been a voice that pointed people to Jesus who is the very righteousness of God. Jesus is the revelation of the righteousness of God and the one that all should unite themselves to. So now we have received righteousness not by works but as a gift.

Paul goes on and declares this righteousness from God comes through faith in Jesus Christ to all who believe. So now we have received righteousness from God as a gift! Mankind has, in different religions, denominations, and theologies, come up with its own idea of righteousness but what we really want to know is how God defines righteousness. God's idea of righteousness is always based on a gift from him. Whenever we think of righteousness we should also remind ourselves that this is a gift. One cannot obtain righteousness by works; therefore, we cannot look at others and blame them for being unrighteous, as that portrays the wrong meaning or idea of righteousness. Righteousness is not earned by our actions; righteousness is actually a gift. This righteousness comes from God through faith in Jesus for all who believe. Paul goes on to say:

This righteousness from God comes through faith in Jesus Christ to all who believe. There is no difference, for all have sinned and fall short of the glory of God, and are justified freely by his grace through the redemption that came by Christ Jesus. **Romans 3:22-24**

Whether you were a Gentile without the covenant of law or you were a Jew with the covenant of law, everyone failed. The Jewish people who failed to live up to the covenant of law could let go of that covenant by leaving it behind them and entering into the New, better Covenant that had already been promised to them so that they can be freely justified by grace.

The Gentiles could leave behind whatever things they were attached to whether it was religion or other worldly ideas and traditions and also enter, as equals, into this eternal covenant of grace and be freely justified. This comes through the redemption of Jesus. Jesus came and did everything on our behalf. What we could never obtain to, Jesus Christ came to establish in our lives by grace. Paul says that:

God presented him as a sacrifice of atonement, through faith in his blood. **Romans 3:25**

The reason God let Jesus come to earth, the reason he allowed him to die upon a cross, the reason for his perfect finished work, and the reason for his forgiveness: the reason for all of this is because God wanted to demonstrate his justice. How did he do this? *He did it through the cross.*

We need to recognise that this is God's understanding of justice. Mankind can come up with all its own ideas about God's justice by defining God as a God of justice who will punish people brutally because of his justice. While it is true that God is a God of justice, the question we must settle in our own hearts and minds is: 'How did God *demonstrate* that very nature of justice?' Paul declares the gospel truth by stating that God demonstrated it by not condemning people but by placing all the condemnation upon his Son on the cross! He did this so that his justice would be perfect and in the perfection of his justice we would see the truth of his mercy for us all.

This is God's idea of justice. Paul was taking the church through a journey of all the terms such as law, righteousness, grace, and justice to help them understand them in the correct way. Having a correct understanding of these words is very important because if we think about these words the wrong way we also think of God and the world around us in the wrong way too.

With the wrong understanding we can easily find ourselves looking at people or nations around us and thinking that "God should judge that person or God should judge that nation." But, actually, God showed us what his justice is. When we look at a person, a group of people, or a nation, we need to understand that God has already put that punishment upon his Son Jesus. It is his kindness that will lead them to repentance. It is God's kindness that is his power. It is not God's hand to punish that is his power; rather, it is his kindness and mercy where his power is manifested. Trying to force people to do what is right through force and punishment didn't work in the Old Covenant and God certainly doesn't try to make that method work in the New Covenant now. It is God's grace and loving kindness that is the almighty power of God to bring transformation in the world and in people's individual lives – in everything. A major reason God sent his Son to earth was to demonstrate to mankind his divine way of justice.

He did this to demonstrate his righteousness, because in his forbearance he had left the sins committed beforehand unpunished —

he did it to demonstrate his righteousness at the present time, so as to
be just and the one who justifies those who have faith in Jesus.
Romans 3:25-26

The whole history of mankind is that the Gentiles were wicked and did terrible things; however, as Paul has highlighted, Israel also did wicked and terrible things, sometimes being even more unrighteous than the Gentiles around them. And so, although Israel had the words of the Bible and could look at them and read them every day, they were, nonetheless, equally unrighteous. God knew that both the Gentile and the Jew could not walk in the ways of God without Christ. They all needed the empowerment of the Sprit within them. Because God knew that mankind, without actually being given the gift of the Spirit, would ultimately fail to live in a way that reflected God's nature, he did not judge them for their sins. Rather, because he had always known his Son would be sent to earth to die for the sins of mankind, he in his foreknowledge did not count their sins against them. However, they did sin and those sins needed to be punished. Because God is just, he did not simply ignore the sins; rather, he made a way for the full penalty of those sins to be justly paid for in the person of Jesus. Upon the cross Jesus took every sin that needs to be justly punished in order that God could then freely justify us by his grace. It is when we see the cross that all our misdeeds were paid for by another, and not just another person but by the divine God himself, that we naturally place our faith in his love for us and declare that Jesus truly is the Lord of Lords.

God continues to demonstrate his justice today. Indeed, God in his forbearance is not counting the sins of anyone against them;[59] but rather, he wants all mankind to see that his Son, through his love for them, already carried their sins upon the cross in order that now they can be justified by the grace of God. Until a person sees the work of Christ, they remain, in their minds, distant from God but God is not far from anyone and he is at work to draw all men to himself through the revelation of Christ upon the cross.

God is just, he is aware of right and wrong, but his justice is revealed in the single moment in history when he put the punishment for those misdeeds upon his Son on the cross. When anyone places their trust in Jesus they enter into the reality of their salvation.

When Christ is lifted up then people naturally want to receive him. When we do the opposite of this which is simply pointing the finger at them and pointing out their sins, what people see are our fingers pointing and condemning them instead of Christ lifted up. They see wagging fingers instead of a glorified Christ.

We know that people need faith in Jesus so they can enter into God's full plan of salvation for them so let us take confidence in that, when we lift Jesus up, he will draw them to himself. Let us not find our message in the wagging of our finger and the pointing out of sins. Let us point to the greatness of Jesus and his love for mankind. Most importantly, let us not try to use the law as a tool to bring about salvation as it actually only brings enslavement. What we can do is lift up Jesus in his glory by praising God that he is the one who justifies us

---

[59] All this is from God, who reconciled us to himself through Christ and gave us the ministry of reconciliation: that God was reconciling the world to himself in Christ, not counting men's sins against them. And he has committed to us the message of reconciliation.
2 Corinthians 5:18-19

and then God will do what he has promised by drawing all mankind to himself.

If we want to see the world transformed by the love of God, we should not waste our time pointing out sins; but rather, we should spend our time lifting up the person of Jesus and boasting in his love. That is what will bring about a transformation in this world. God has presented to all of mankind the truth of his justice, that it is a gift, just as righteousness is, which comes through faith in Jesus. For this reason, no one can boast about their own righteousness because no one earned it by their own zeal and efforts. Instead, we can give our attention to boasting solely in the Lord.

Where, then, is boasting? It is excluded. On what principle? On that of observing the law? No, but on that of faith. For we maintain that a man is justified by faith apart from observing the law. **Romans 3:27-28**

It's interesting that Paul made these remarks after the Galatian church disaster (of rejecting the gospel of grace and deciding to believe the false gospel that yoked them under a mixed covenant of law and grace) that had taken place. They rejected the gospel that Paul had preached to them. Also, in Corinth, where most of the church misunderstood the gospel and used it as an excuse to say everything they were doing was okay, including sexual immortality, Paul came back to them and still preached from the position of seeing them in their new creation reality. He preached they were new creations. Their bodies were the temple of the Holy Spirit. They were holy and blameless. He understood he didn't need to point out their sins. He needed to point out who they were in Christ. Paul believed that when they truly believed the truth about who they were in Christ and what he had done for them then sin would lose its power and righteousness would be glorified in their lives. People could point to Paul and call him out as a phony and a fake, pointing to his churches that were in a mess, and highlight all his failings. Paul's position regarding this matter was that regardless of these failings 'we' maintain that a man is justified by faith apart from law. Paul said 'we' because Paul ultimately represented God's movement of believers who stood up, as Paul did, for the truth of the gospel. There were a lot of believers that were partnering with Paul in the same wonderful truth of the gospel.

Paul understood that some were obviously misunderstanding the gospel he preached just as some were clearly still living with sinful actions. He understood that his church communities were being slandered by the false preachers who created churches that, at the very least, presented themselves religiously polished on the outside. Regardless of the shortcomings of Paul, or the churches that he founded, he maintained that the gospel is the good news of a righteousness by faith apart from law. Why did he do it? Because it is, quite simply, the gospel. It is the very essence of the gospel. It is the truth of God made known to mankind.

It's the good news of God's grace that Christ has declared us to be righteous and not through our works but through our faith in him. That he has justified us freely by his grace and it comes through his redemption and not through our works. Paul maintained that we are now, in Christ, in right standing with God. We are loved by God, we are walking with God, God is pleased with us, and God sees us as holy and righteous. This is all by faith in Jesus Christ and apart from any attempts to observe the law.

It is these bold statements of Paul that continue to cause controversy in Christian circles today as many still hold to the wrong understanding of righteousness; therefore, naturally also misunderstanding the message that seeks to reveal the truth about righteousness. The problem is that many in the church in Paul's day believed that righteousness was obtained through the following the written instructions in the Scriptures so for Paul to say the church community could live without the law was, in their mind, to say they could live without righteousness. To believe this is to believe the false understanding of both the law and righteousness completely.

The law is not a tool for righteousness. In fact, if you look to it as a tool to help you be righteous by your efforts, it will actually become a tool for unrighteousness in your life.

The law was a voice in the wilderness to Israel to ultimately lead people to Jesus. It was a John the Baptist type ministry, a testimony that led people to Jesus by speaking about the coming Christ and promoting that Christ as the one everyone should follow in order to truly live. The law, like John the Baptist, leads people to the one through whom they can enter into the New Covenant of grace. It is not and should never be thought of as a teacher of right living.

CONCLUSION
LOVE IS THE WAY (NOT LAW)

"Do we, then, nullify the law by this faith? Not at all! Rather, we uphold the law." **Romans 3:31**

In conclusion to all that Paul has shared, he makes this final point in what has become perhaps the most misquoted Scripture in the Bible. Whenever Romans 3:31 is quoted, it must be discussed in context to the whole letter. It is disturbing that people will take one verse and build an entire doctrine upon it that defends the notion that we, as Christians, are still under the law and should be proud to be yoked to the law even though the entire letter is written to explain to us that we are not under the law at all! It can't be any clearer really. The entire letter of Romans is testifying to this one point. So then, why did Paul write this statement?

What I have shared with you throughout this book is that Paul's main purpose was to explain the correct way to understand the law and to be aware how easily it can be misunderstood. The false way of understanding the law is to view it as a written code of rules we can follow in order to be considered righteous. Let's be very clear here in saying this is the false understanding of the law. Paul, however, loved the law in its correct understanding as a testimony to God's promise to give mankind a Saviour through whom we can receive, as a gift, the righteousness of God. So when Paul makes this comment, *"Do we nullify the law? Not at all! Rather, we uphold the law,"* he is not suggesting we uphold the law as a written code of moral instructions that, when read and quoted, will empower us live a righteous life; rather, he is saying we can uphold its true purpose which is a testimony to the promise of Christ whom we have now joyfully received. We don't *nullify* the testimony of our Saviour; rather, we *uphold* the testimony of our Saviour. If we take a quick look forward into chapter nine we read Paul testifying to these two different perspectives regarding the law:

What then shall we say? That the Gentiles, who did not pursue righteousness, have obtained it, a righteousness that is by faith; but the people of Israel, who pursued the law as the way of righteousness, have not attained their goal. Why not? Because they pursued it not by faith but as if it were by works. They stumbled over the stumbling stone. As it is written: "See, I lay in Zion a stone that causes people to stumble and a rock that makes them fall, and the one who believes in him will never be put to shame. **Romans 9:30-33**

Paul talks about how those who tried to understand the law as a rule book to acquire righteousness failed to obtain righteousness and yet those who were not looking to the law as a written code to acquire righteousness ended up receiving the righteousness of God. Why did that happen? It happened because the Gentiles received righteousness as a gift. The Israelites, who worked to obtain righteousness, failed. Why? They failed because they tried to earn it by their good works. They stumbled over Jesus who, is the stumbling stone to so many religious people, because they were trying to earn what is, in actual fact, only ever received as a gift. Those who want to earn right standing before God end up tripping over the grace of God all the time and become bitter about God's grace as if it is a frustrating rock that interferes in their religious ambition to produce righteousness themselves.

Again, when we read the above Scripture, in context, the fullness of the law in its correct understanding is fulfilled in the reality of God's love. Christ in us allows us to stop pointing the finger and judging both others and ourselves. With that freedom we can then spend our time focussed on love.

God's heart is a heart of love and God is leading people to Christ through his heart of love. Even when we look into the Old Testament we find that God did not rebuke his people for failing to fulfil legalistic rules or ceremonial obligations. Actually they loved to do all those things but their problem was they didn't actually love people. They loved the rules but failed to love others. God, on the other hand, never enjoyed the ceremonial obligations or the legalistic rules. They were given as a shadow of Christ; however, in and of themselves, they greatly frustrated God because he saw how his people were taking hold of them as if they were the reality whereas God always wanted them to see the higher reality of love.

The law itself is good and holy in its correct understanding; however, when we think of the law as a moral written code that, when followed, will make us moral and righteous people we end up upholding the law in its false understanding, bringing unnecessary condemnation on us and others who see us upholding the false understanding of the law. Paul implores us that what we need to do is live with the revelation that *'a righteousness apart from the law has been made known'* and yet we can still joyfully uphold the law because the true understanding of the law is a 'prophet like' voice testifying to the grace of Jesus.

Paul encourages the church that we are not nullifying the law by saying we now live by grace alone; rather, by saying that we now live by the Spirit of grace we are in fact upholding the law! To uphold the law is to believe what it says regarding the promise of Jesus and the New Covenant freely given apart from the Old Covenant written code of law.

Some preachers love to quote Romans 3:31 as if it proves and justifies their theology to keep Christians yoked under the law but what they are in fact doing is attaching the false understanding of the law to this Scripture. Romans 3:31 should not be quoted or used to define a theology without also quoting Romans 3:21 with it. Let's look quickly at the two verses together:

"But now apart from the law the righteousness of God has been made known, to which the Law and the Prophets testify." **Romans 3:21**

"Do we, then, nullify the law by this faith? Not at all rather, we uphold the law." **Romans 3:31**

We don't nullify the law because we are doing exactly what it testified to. He have embraced Christ, entered into the New Covenant, and now live by God's Spirit that will naturally lead us into all his ways of love. If we fail to understand, or stubbornly refuse to accept, the true purpose of the law then we will never understand what Paul meant, not only regarding this verse, but in everything he wrote about.

We uphold the law because the law is upholding a righteousness by faith apart from the law. When our righteousness is measured by a rule book, it causes us to consistently doubt if we are truly righteous and focuses our thoughts on our works; however, when our righteousness is measured by the Son of God it causes us to continually believe and place our focus on consistently on Jesus. Why should we doubt when Christ's work upon the cross was perfect and that is the work that defines our righteousness.

That place of rest in our spirit allows us to walk in all that God desires because we are not living in the shadows of inner fear, or hiding from the weight of condemnation, but, rather, we are living in the light of Christ's finished work which allows us to walk in his ways without worry because Christ is our righteousness.

When people talk about upholding the law, we can agree this is good to do but we must do it in its correct understanding. Uphold it in its correct way. Uphold it knowing that it testifies to the New Covenant of grace apart from an instruction like rule book known as the written code. This means we won't be pointing out people's lack and weakness but the One who came to be their strength and give them his fullness. Righteousness has *nothing* to do with a legalistic list of rules found in a written format and *everything* to do with the Son of God who came to earth to impart to us the gift of his righteousness.

Paul was helping the early church in Rome to be established in the correct understanding of righteousness. He took them on a journey to recognise that while it was evident that the Gentile world without a covenant of law was unrighteous so too was Israel, who had a covenant of law, unrighteous. He showed them that what is written in the law about unrighteousness was actually written to those who were under it in order to highlight the fact that even with a written code there is no power to actually outwork a righteous life by one's own will power and determination.

Paul clarified how it is not the law that makes someone righteous. On the contrary, being under the law makes one unrighteous. Without a covenant one will be equally unrighteous. But how then does one actually be righteous? This was the whole point of all that Paul wrote. This is the point he wanted to church to really understand. Righteousness is a gift that is given through faith. It is a gift by the grace of God and not earned by our good works.

Righteousness is a gift and it is therefore guaranteed to us all. For we have all fallen short of God's glory by our works and we are all justified, apart from our works, by the grace of God and this is what brings God glory. Grace is the empowerment of God. God's righteousness is available to all who believe. It allows us to rest and understand that we truly are righteous because Jesus is our righteousness. He has become, by the working of his grace, our holiness, righteousness, and redemption.

We don't try to hold up the law thinking of it as a list of laws that will move people to live a righteous life. We uphold it when we use it to point out the Christ who has been given to the world so he could now give us the gift of righteousness.

Paul never backed away from clarifying this truth. He didn't twist or ignore Scripture in order to preach grace; rather, he loved the Scriptures and he understood and used them correctly in the light of Christ. That is why Paul could testify that regarding the Law and the Prophets he had a clear conscious. When he preached the Good news of God's grace apart from law, he was simply preaching the exact message the Law and the Prophets themselves testified to.

So, just as the law proclaims, lay hold of Jesus and embrace God's grace. You can trust him. The law's job is now done. You have now received Christ and so freely go and live in Christ who is your inheritance. Enjoy the Spirit and the obedience that you have longed for. God's grace is more than enough to outwork the empowered life through the Spirit of God which was given to you through Christ, your King, your Love, your Saviour, your Holiness, your Righteousness, your Redemption, and your Empowerment from God.

Righteousness is a beautiful thing; it is a gift of God. Jesus is our gift and he continues to live in and through us. He empowers us to live a life of obedience by faith. Christ in us will outwork an active righteousness in our lives not through a wagging finger but through hearts of grace. For living by the Spirit of grace will lead people to be drawn to Jesus. And then, as people are drawn to Jesus, they too can receive the gift of God that he desires to give all mankind. The law is a servant that testifies of the Saviour of the world. Like John the Baptist, the law desires people to let go of their desire to be a 'disciple of the law' and instead follow the Spirit of Christ. Living a life that is led by the Spirit is every Christian's calling. It is the desire of God's heart and a glorious honour we are blessed to partake in. Enjoy it.

"Look! The Lamb of God, who takes away the sins of the world. He must become greater and I must become less. Follow him!"

OTHER BOOKS BY MICK MOONEY

Non-Fiction

Look! The Finished Work Of Jesus

Paraphrase (Ephesians, Philippians, Colossians, Philemon)

The Gospel Cannot Be Chained

Comic Book

Searching For Grace: Joining The Church

For more information visit:

www.searchingforgrace.com

Acknowledgements

I would like to take this opportunity to thank my wonderful wife Mira for her continual support and understanding. Thank you for always being so full of grace and love, God knows I need it. You are my shinning star and I love you dearly.

Special thanks to Mrs. Sherry Lynn Stewart De Haven who graciously helped proof read and edit the manuscript. Your help came at the perfect time and you did a wonderful job. Thank you.

Thanks to all my friends who helped bring this project to completion through reading and reviewing this book, and for all the great and valuable feedback you gave me throughout the process.

Finally, I would like to thank everyone who continues to read and share my work. I appreciate every one of you. Thank you for allowing me to be part of your journey.

Blue skies,

Mick

God's Grace
Apart From Law

A conversational journey through the first three chapters of Paul's letter to the Romans

Mick Mooney

Published by Lightview Media

LIGHTVIEW MEDIA

CPSIA information can be obtained
at www.ICGtesting.com
Printed in the USA
BVHW03s1431200518
516788BV00008B/72/P

9 783943 229035